Marius Fredheim

Copula Methods in Finance

Marius Fredheim

Copula Methods in Finance

VDM Verlag Dr. Müller

Imprint

Bibliographic information by the German National Library: The German National Library lists this publication at the German National Bibliography; detailed bibliographic information is available on the Internet at http://dnb.d-nb.de.

Cover image: www.purestockx.com

Publisher:
VDM Verlag Dr. Müller Aktiengesellschaft & Co. KG , Dudweiler Landstr. 125 a, 66123 Saarbrücken, Germany,
Phone +49 681 9100-698, Fax +49 681 9100-988,
Email: info@vdm-verlag.de

Zugl.: Bergen, University of Bergen, Diss., 2007

Produced in USA and UK by:
Lightning Source Inc., La Vergne, Tennessee, USA
Lightning Source UK Ltd., Milton Keynes, UK
BookSurge LLC, 5341 Dorchester Road, Suite 16, North Charleston, SC 29418, USA

ISBN: 978-3-639-06814-6

Acknowledgements

I thank my supervisor, professor Dag Tjøstheim, for giving me the opportunity to work with this interesting topic in my own way. His help and support during this time has meant a lot to me.

Further, thanks are due to my fellow student (now Ph.D. student), Karl Ove Hufthammer, for reading my manuscript and suggesting improvements. I also thank him for his support with Linux, LaTeX 2_ε and the statistical package R. His technical enthusiasm has been an inspiration for me during my studies.

Finally, I thank Hilde Holmefjord and our two sons. This thesis could not have been written without their support.

Bergen, 1st June 2007
Marius Fredheim

Contents

2

1

Introduction

Copulas provide us with a tool for constructing multivariate distributions with arbitrary marginal distributions and a wide range of dependence structures.

The aim of this thesis is to describe what the practitioner, or scientist, needs to know about copulas. Although the emphasis is on financial applications, the general theory is relevant for any multivariate setting.

The outline of the thesis is as follows. Chapter 2 is a discussion of multivariate distribution functions that are useful for financial data. We emphasize that the normality assumption does not hold for daily and monthly returns from stocks. In chapter 3 we proceed with a discussion of commonly used dependence measures, and we highlight deficiencies of the correlation coefficient.

We start chapter 4 by describing the properties a general function must satisfy in order to be a copula and goes on by describing the properties of the most common copulas.

In chapter 5 we discuss the problem of estimating the parameters in a copula and in chapter 6 we review the recent goodness-of-fit procedures suggested in the literature. Note that goodness-of-fit procedures for copulas is an area of research where no single best procedure has been agreed upon.

Chapter 7 is a short review of some of the main applications of copulas in relation to credit risk models.

Software

All simulations have been done using the statistical package R, version 2.5.0. (R Development Core Team 2007).

We have used the following R packages. The `copula` package (Yan 2007) was used to simulate from copulas and to estimate parameters. We used the package `mvtnorm` (Genz *et al.* 2006) to simulate from the multivariate normal and the multivariate *t*-distribution. To perform the normality tests we used the package `nortest` (Gross 2003). For scatterplots in 3 dimensions we used `scatterplot3d` (Ligges and Mächler 2003). For making PostScript® files we used `Hmisc` (Harrell Jr. 2007).

2

Distribution functions

The aim of this chapter is to review some of the standard facts of the most common multivariate distributions. In section 2.2 on page 6 we examine the basic properties of the normal distribution, and in section 2.2.1 on page 8 we examine the fact that daily and monthly returns from stocks do not, in general, follow a multivariate normal distribution. The tails are too thin and the probability of *joint* extreme outcomes is too low.

In section 2.3 on page 12 we introduce some alternative distributions in the class of normal mixture models. These distributions have proved to be very useful in financial modelling and provide a good alternative to the usual normal distribution. But still, all the multivariate distributions we examine in this chapter forces the one-dimensional marginal distributions to be in the same class of univariate distributions. This is only satisfactory if we have a portfolio of reasonable homogeneous assets, that is, a portfolio where it is reasonable to assume that the marginal distributions are of the same type.

This chapter is based on several textbooks. More in-depth introductions to multivariate analysis can be found in Johnson and Wichern (2002), who use the standard normal assumption, Joe (1997) who treats non-normal random variables and McNeil *et al.* (2005, chapter 3) for financial applications.

2.1 Random vectors and their distributions

Since we work with multivariate data, we need to introduce the random vector. A random vector is simply a vector whose elements are random variables, or more formally: A random vector is a function from a sample space Ω into $\mathbb{R}^d$, where $\mathbb{R}$ denote the real line $(-\infty, \infty)$ and $\mathbb{R}^d$ denote the d-space $\mathbb{R} \times \cdots \times \mathbb{R}$.

Note on notation: Random variables will be denoted with uppercase letters and realized values of a variable will be denoted by the corresponding lowercase letter.

Consider a d-dimensional random vector $\boldsymbol{X} = (X_1, \ldots, X_d)'$. The distribution of $\boldsymbol{X}$ is described by the joint distribution function, written $F_{\boldsymbol{X}}(\boldsymbol{x})$, or simply F.

$$F_{\boldsymbol{X}}(\boldsymbol{x}) = P(\boldsymbol{X} \leq \boldsymbol{x}) = P(X_1 \leq x_1, \ldots, X_d \leq x_d). \tag{2.1}$$

This joint distribution function tells us which values the variable can assume, and how often it assumes them; in other words, it completely describes the probability of occurrence over its domain. The joint distribution function also determines the distribution of subsets of $\boldsymbol{X}$ and thereby the marginal distributions of the elements in $\boldsymbol{X}$. Consequently, if we are interested in the distribution of the random variables X_i individually, we can compute the marginal distribution function, written F_{X_i}, or just F_i, from the joint distribution function. For all i we have

$$F_{X_i}(x_i) = P(X_i \leq x_i) = F(\infty, \ldots, \infty, x_i, \infty, \ldots, \infty), \tag{2.2}$$

and, when it exists, we will refer to the derivative of F_{X_i} as the marginal density of X_i, written f_{X_i}, or simply f_i. The k-dimensional marginal distributions are defined in a similar way by fixing fewer variables.

It is clear from equation 2.2 that the joint distribution function of $\boldsymbol{X}$ contains all the information about the marginals, but on the other hand, knowledge about the marginal distributions of X_1 to X_d do *not* determine their joint distribution. Consequently, the joint distribution function contains more information than the marginals. In chapter 4 we will see that this additional information is captured by the functions which are the main topic of this thesis, namely the copulas.

Some useful transformations

In this section we present some useful transformations we will come across repeatedly, namely; the generalized inverse, the probability integral transformation and the quantile transformation.

We start with the definition of the generalized inverse. Since a distribution function F_X can be constant on some interval, say $[x_1, x_2]$, the usual inverse, F_X^{-1}, is not well defined: x in $[x_1, x_2]$ satisfies $F_X(x) = u$. We can avoid this problem by defining the generalized inverse.

Definition 2.1.1: Generalized inverse

The generalized inverse $F_i^{\leftarrow}$ of the distribution F_i is defined as:

$$F_i^{\leftarrow}(u) = \inf\{x : F_i(x) \geq u\}, \quad \text{for all } u \text{ in } [0, 1]. \tag{2.3}$$

When F_i is strictly increasing and continuous, we see that $F_i^{\leftarrow} = F_i^{-1}$. In situations like this we will use the notation of the usual inverse.

Another well known and useful theorem is the probability integral transformation.

Theorem 2.1.2: Probability integral transformation

Let X have a continuous distribution function F_X and define the random variable U as $U = F_X(X)$. Then U is uniformly distributed on $[0, 1]$, that is, $P(U \leq u) = u$, for $0 \leq u \leq 1$.

Last, we present the quantile transformation, a well known tool in simulations.

Lemma 2.1.3: Quantile transformation

Let X have a distribution function $F_X(x)$. If $U \sim U(0, 1)$ has a standard uniform distribution, then $\mathbb{P}(F_X^{\leftarrow}(U) \leq x) = F_X(x)$.

Consequently, by generating a random number U, between 0 and 1, and solving for x in the equation $F_X(x) = u$, we can generate an observation x from a population with distribution function F_X.

2.2 The multivariate normal distribution

The normal distribution is the most widely used distribution. It plays a fundamental role in multivariate analysis and financial theory. Below we give a definition of the multivariate normal distribution through its density.

Definition 2.2.1: Multivariate normal distribution

The random variables in $X = (X_1, X_2, \ldots, X_d)'$ have a multivariate normal distribution if their joint probability density function f is given by

$$f(x) = \frac{1}{\sqrt{(2\pi)^d |\Sigma|}} \exp\{-\frac{1}{2}(x - \mu)'\Sigma^{-1}(x - \mu)\}, \quad x \in \mathbb{R}^d, \qquad (2.4)$$

where x is a d dimensional vector of values, μ is the d dimensional vector of means, Σ is the $d \times d$ covariance matrix assumed to have full rank d, and $|\Sigma|$ is the determinant of Σ.

Clearly, the distribution is characterized by μ and Σ and it will be denoted $N_d(\mu, \Sigma)$. It is common to denote the distribution function F of the standard normal distribution by the Greek letter Φ. We will adopt this practice, and we will use the bold letter Φ to denote a multivariate standard normal distribution function.

In figure 2.1 on the facing page we have a simulation from the 3-dimensional standard normal distribution with correlation 0.5 between all the variables.

Properties of the multivariate normal distribution

The (multivariate) normal distribution is often a good approximation for the true population distribution. If we, as an example, draw a histogram of variables like weight and height of 100 randomly chosen students we will probably recognize the famous bell curve. In situations like this the normal assumption is plausible. No singel observation like a very tall or heavy person will dramatically change the sample mean or variance.

Second, with the help of the the central limit theorem, we know that the distribution of many multivariate statistics are approximately normal. The central limit theorem states that for a large random sample from a distribution with mean μ and finite variance σ^2 the distribution of the sample mean $\overline{X}$ is approximately normally distributed. With no other assumptions than independence and finite variance, we end up with normality.

The 3–dimensional normal distribution

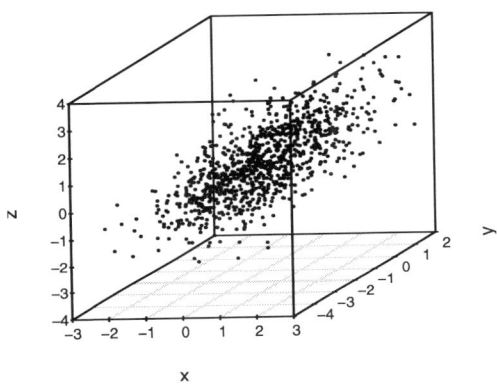

Figure 2.1: A plot of 1,000 simulated points from the 3-dimensional standard normal distribution with pairwise correlation 0.5.

In addition to this the normal distribution has some nice mathematical properties. The following are true for a random vector X that follows a multivariate normal distribution:

1. Linear combinations of the components of X are normally distributed.
2. All subsets of the components of X has (multivariate) normal distributions.
3. Zero covariance implies that the corresponding components are independent.
4. The conditional distributions of the components are (multivariate) normal.

Finally, another important property of the normal distribution is that the sample mean $\overline{X}$ and sample covariance matrix S captures all the information about $\Theta = (\mu, \Sigma)$ contained in the sample. Consequently, if we can assume a normal distribution, the common practice of summarizing a data set by reporting only the mean and variance is justified. But, if the data cannot be regarded as (multivariate) normal, techniques that depend on $\overline{X}$ and S may be ignoring useful sample information.

Elliptical distributions

We see from the multivariate normal density given in equation 2.4 on page 6 that points with equal density lie on ellipsoids determined by equations of the form $(x - \mu)'\Sigma^{-1}(x - \mu) = c$. Whenever a multivariate density $f(x)$ depends only on x through the quadratic form $(x - \mu)'\Sigma^{-1}(x - \mu)$, we say that it is a density of an elliptical distribution. The multivariate t and other normal variance mixture distributions, to be defined in definition 2.3.1 on page 13, are examples of elliptical distributions.

Many of the properties of the multivariate normal distribution can be generalized to the wider class of elliptical distributions. If we can find a substitute to the normal distribution in the class of elliptical distributions, it is still sensible to use the linear correlation as a dependence measure and apply standard approaches, like Value at Risk and Markowitz portfolio theory, in risk management. See Campbell *et al.* (1997) and Embrechts *et al.* (2002) for further details.

Fallacies

As Embrechts *et al.* (2002) stress, we have to be careful if we can not be sure that the data follows a multivariate normal distribution. He points out that

1. The fact that two or more random variables $X_1, \ldots, X_d$ follows a *univariate* normal distribution does not imply that $X = (X_1, \ldots, X_d)$ follow a *multivariate* normal distribution.
2. Knowledge of the marginal distributions and the correlation does not in general determine the joint distribution. See figure 4.6 on page 52 for examples of different bivariate distributions with identical marginals and correlation.

For futher details and other fallacies we recommend Embrechts *et al.* (2002).

2.2.1 Testing the normality assumption

There are overwhelming evidence against the normal assumption in real financial data: the tails are fatter and the dependence is not fully captured by the covariance matrix. We will explore this further in section 2.2.1 on the facing page, where we test the normality assumption on returns from different stocks and on some stock market indices.

In our test we have tried to combine formal and informal procedures. By plotting the time series and by using a histogram, a boxplot and a QQ-plot we get a good overview of the properties of the marginals in the sample. But even though the exploratory tools are useful, we need to test the normality assumption more formally.

There exists several formal tests of multivariate and univariate normality, all with different properties. McNeil *et al.* (2005) recommend using the Mardias or Shapiro Wilks test to test the multivariate normality assumption, and the Anderson-Darlings or Jarque-Bera test to test the univariate normality assumption. These tests are implemented in most statistical software and are easy to use.

Normality in daily and monthly returns from stocks

In this section we investigate the assumption of normality in daily and monthly returns from several stocks, namely Statoil (STO), General motors (GM), Intel Corporation (INTEL) and International Business Machines (IBM). The market portfolio consists of three American indices, American Stock Exchange (AMEX), NASDAQ and the New York Stock Exchange (NYSE). In addition to this we have included the daily returns from Oslo Stock Exchange (OSE) in the univariate test of normality in daily return series.

The data we consider consists of four years of daily return series, spanning 2001 to 2006, and ten years of monthly return series, spanning 1996 to 2006. The data are collected from the Center for Research in Security Prices (CRSP) and Net Fonds.

Univariate tests: For each return series we applied three tests of univariate normality, the Anderson-Darling, Cramer von Mises and Jarque-Bera test. In table 2.1 on the next page we see that the tests rejected the normality assumption for the daily returns, but not for the monthly returns. This result is supported by the exploratory tools.

In figure 2.2 on page 11 we see a QQ normality plot of the daily and the monthly returns from IBM. Note that we have used return series spanning the same time period, 1996–2006. We clearly see that the QQ-plot for the daily return series shows the usual inverted 'S-shape', which suggests that the tails are too heavy compared to the normal distribution. We do not find this shape

Daily returns			**Monthly returns**		
Stock	Test	P	Stock	Test	P
OSE	Anderson-Darling	0.00	Market	Anderson-Darling	0.25
	Cramer von Mises	0.00		Cramer von Mises	0.43
	Jarque-Bera	0.00		Jarque-Bera	0.01
STO	Anderson-Darling	0.00	STO	Anderson-Darling	0.54
	Cramer von Mises	0.00		Cramer von Mises	0.43
	Jarque-Bera	0.00		Jarque-Bera	NA
GM	Anderson-Darling	0.00	GM	Anderson-Darling	0.11
	Cramer von Mises	0.00		Cramer von Mises	0.16
	Jarque-Bera	0.00		Jarque-Bera	0.38
INTC	Anderson-Darling	0.00	INTC	Anderson-Darling	0.25
	Cramer von Mises	0.00		Cramer von Mises	0.31
	Jarque-Bera	0.00		Jarque-Bera	0.13
IBM	Anderson-Darling	0.00	IBM	Anderson-Darling	0.07
	Cramer von Mises	0.00		Cramer von Mises	0.06
	Jarque-Bera	0.00		Jarque-Bera	0.01

(a) Daily returns from February 2001 to 2006, $n = 1,140$.

(b) Monthly returns from 1996 to 2006, $n = 120$.

Table 2.1: P-values from three univariate normality tests applied to different return series. The monthly return series appear to follow a univariate normal distribution, while daily return series do not satisfy the normality assumption. See section 2.2.1 for details.

in the QQ-plot of the monthly returns. This indicates that monthly returns do not behave as 'wildly' as daily returns.

Multivariate test: To test for multivariate normality it is not enough to test that the univariate margins are normal. We need to test for *joint* normality. When we perform Shapiro-Wilks multivariate normality test on the monthly returns from STO, GM, INTEL and IBM we get a P-value of 0.017. This rejects the multivariate normality assumption for the monthly returns as well.

Since there are some evidence that the univariate distribution of the monthly returns follow a normal distribution, the rejection of the multivariate normality assumption indicates that the multivariate normal distribution do not have the

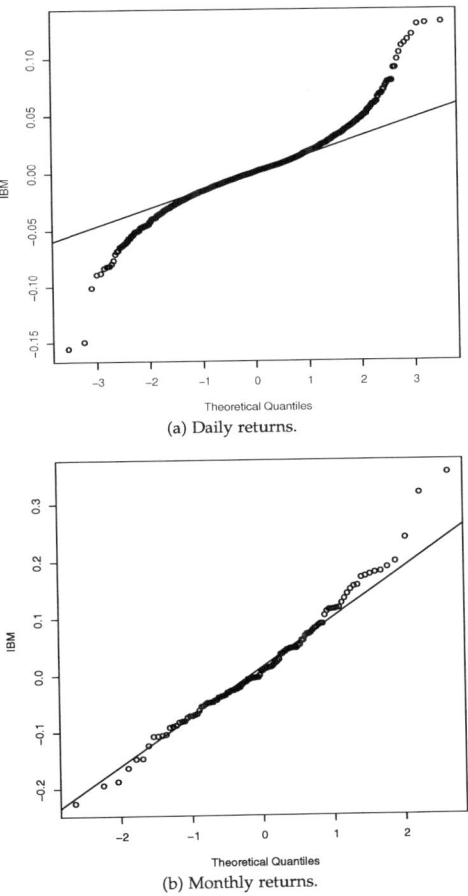

(a) Daily returns.

(b) Monthly returns.

Figure 2.2: QQ-plot of the daily and monthly returns from the IBM share from 1996 to 2006.

right dependence structure; it does not assign enough weight to *joint* extreme outcomes.

Conclusion: We have seen that the univariate, and therefore the multivariate, normality assumption is rejected in the daily return series. For the monthly return series the assumption of univariate normality looks more reasonable, but still the test of *multivariate* normality rejects the null-hypothesis.

We point out that this is an example with a few, not randomly chosen, stocks. But, more in-depth studies verifies that daily, weekly and monthly return data do not satisfy the normal assumption. However, for return series over longer time intervals, like a quarter of a year or longer, there are some evidence that the return series are close to being normally distributed. This may be due to a central limit effect when the data are aggregated.

2.3 Normal mixture distributions

Since it is well-known that return series from stocks do not follow a multivariate normal distribution, we need to search for alternatives. The class of normal mixture distributions has turned out to be very useful in financial modelling.

The normal mixture distributions are generalizations of the multivariate normal distributions. It is clear that $X = (X_1, \ldots, X_d)'$ has a multivariate normal distribution if

$$X = \mu + AZ, \tag{2.5}$$

where $Z = (Z_1, \ldots, Z_k)'$ is a vector of independent and identically distributed univariate standard normal random variables, A is a $d \times k$ matrix of constants and μ, the mean vector, is a d dimensional vector of constants. We concentrate on the case where $\text{rank}(A) = d \leq k$ so that the covariance matrix $\Sigma = AA'$ has full rank d and is invertible and positive definite.

The main idea behind the normal mixture models is that we can put randomness in the covariance matrix to obtain normal variance mixtures, and then in the mean vector as well to obtain normal mean-variance mixtures. As we will see below, the multivariate t and the generalized hyperbolic distributions are special cases of the normal mixture distributions. These distributions are known to give a good fit to financial return series. For more details about normal mixture distributions and their applications in finance, see McNeil *et al.* (2005), Bingham and Kiesel (2002) and Eberlein and Keller (1995).

2.3.1 Normal variance mixtures

Definition 2.3.1: Normal variance mixtures

The random vector $X = (X_1, \ldots, X_d)'$ is said to have a normal variance mixture distribution if

$$X \overset{\mathrm{D}}{=} \mu + \sqrt{W}AZ, \tag{2.6}$$

where $\overset{\mathrm{D}}{=}$ means equal in distribution, and

- $Z \sim N_k(\mathbf{0}, I_k)$,
- $W \geq 0$ is an non-negative random variable, independent of Z, and
- $A \in \mathbb{R}^{d \times k}$ and $\mu \in \mathbb{R}^d$ are a matrix and a vector of constants, respectively.

Since $X_1, \ldots, X_d$ depend on the same random variable W, we see that uncorrelated normal variance mixtures are independent if and only if W is a constant. This is reasonable; if W is *big* we expect the values in X to be *big* and vice verca.

Multivariate *t*-distribution

Let Z have a standard normal distribution $Z \sim N(0,1)$ and let V be a chi-squared variable with ν degrees of freedom, $V \sim \chi^2_\nu$. Further suppose that Z and V are independent. Then it is known from basic statistics, see for instance Casella and Berger (2002, page 222), that

$$\frac{Z}{\sqrt{V/\nu}} \sim t_\nu, \tag{2.7}$$

where t_ν denotes the univariate t distribution with ν degrees of freedom.

The statement above can be generalized to a multivariate t-distribution. The random vector $X = (X_1, \ldots, X_n)'$ is said to have a multivariate t-distribution if

$$X = \mu + \frac{Z}{\sqrt{V/\nu}}, \tag{2.8}$$

where $Z \sim N_d(\mathbf{0}, \Sigma)$ is independent of $V \sim \chi^2_\nu$. This is equivalent to W, from equation 2.6, having an inverse gamma distribution $W \sim \mathrm{Ig}(\frac{\nu}{2}, \frac{\nu}{2})$, described in section A.1 on page 101.

We denote the d-dimensional t distribution with v degrees of freedom by $t_d(\boldsymbol{\mu}, \boldsymbol{\Sigma}, v)$. Its density is given by

$$f(\boldsymbol{x}) = \frac{\Gamma(\frac{v+d}{2})}{\Gamma(\frac{v}{2})(\pi v)^{\frac{d}{2}}|\boldsymbol{\Sigma}|^{\frac{1}{2}}} \left(1 + \frac{(\boldsymbol{x}-\boldsymbol{\mu})'\boldsymbol{\Sigma}^{-1}(\boldsymbol{x}-\boldsymbol{\mu})}{v}\right)^{\frac{-(v+d)}{2}}, \tag{2.9}$$

where, we note that $\boldsymbol{\Sigma} = \boldsymbol{A}\boldsymbol{A}'$ is the covariance matrix of $\boldsymbol{A}\boldsymbol{Z}$. The covariance matrix of $\boldsymbol{X}$ will be $\frac{v}{v-2}\boldsymbol{\Sigma}$ for $v > 2$. Otherwise, the covariance of $\boldsymbol{X}$ is not defined. For details see McNeil *et al.* (2005, pages 73–75)

Clearly points with equal density lie on ellipsoids determined by equations of the form $(\boldsymbol{x}-\boldsymbol{\mu})'\boldsymbol{\Sigma}^{-1}(\boldsymbol{x}-\boldsymbol{\mu}) = c$. Consequently, it is an elliptical distribution.

Since $X_1, \ldots, X_n$ all depend on the same random variable W, uncorrelated multivariate t-distributed random variables are dependent, and, for the same reason, all the marginals are forced to have the same degrees of freedom parameter v.

We also remark that the multivariate Cauchy distribution is a special case of the multivariate t-distribution with $v < 2$.

The 3–dimensional t–distribution

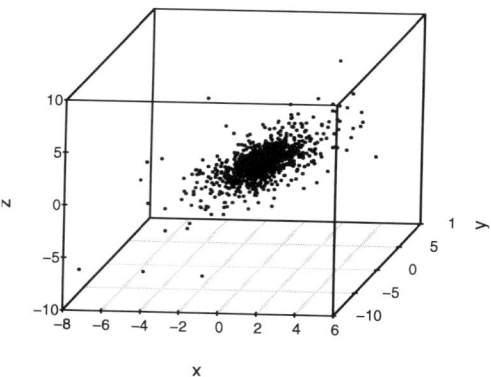

Figure 2.3: A plot of 1,000 simulated points from the 3-dimensional standard t-distribution with pairwise correlation 0.5 and 4 degrees of freedom.

In figure 2.3 on the facing page we see a simulation from the 3-dimensional standard t-distribution with correlation 0.5 and 4 degrees of freedom. Compared to the 3-dimensional normal distribution in figure 2.1 on page 7 it is clear that the t-distribution gives room for simultaneous extreme observation. This supports the use of the t-distribution to model return series from stocks.

2.3.2 Normal mean-variance mixtures

All the distributions we have considered so far are symmetric around μ and it follows directly from the definition of symmetry that the marginals are marginally symmetric (see section A.2 on page 101.). This may be an oversimplified model for return data, since it is sometimes claimed that negative stock returns have heavier tails than positive stock returns. We could not find support for this in the stocks we investigated.

If we in addition put randomness in the mean as well as in the variance, we get the normal mean-variance mixtures. These distributions allow for nonsymmetry.

Definition 2.3.2: Normal mean-variance mixtures

The random vector $X = (X_1, \ldots, X_d)'$ is said to have a normal mean-variance mixture distribution if

$$X \overset{\mathrm{D}}{=} m(W) + \sqrt{W} A Z, \tag{2.10}$$

where $\overset{\mathrm{D}}{=}$ means equal in distribution, and

- $Z \sim N_k(\mathbf{0}, I_k)$,
- $W \geq 0$ is an non-negative random variable, independent of Z,
- $A \in \mathbb{R}^{d \times k}$ is a matrix, and
- $m : [0, \infty) \to \mathbb{R}^d$ is a measurable function.

A special case of the normal mean-variance mixtures is the generalized hyperbolic distribution obtained when W has a generalized inverse Gaussian distribution. The generalized hyperbolic distribution is generalized in the sense that it contains the hyperbolic distribution, the normal inverse Gaussian (NIG) distribution, the variance-gamma distribution and the skewed t-distribution. These distributions provide good alternatives for the normal distribution in financial applications. For more details, see McNeil *et al.* (2005, pages 78–88) and the references therein.

2.4 Extreme value distributions

Extreme value theory (EVT) is a relative new area of study, but it has developed to be an important part of statistics. Since multivariate extreme value theory is related to copulas, and since EVT still is an unknown subject to many researchers, we will give a short introduction.

2.4.1 Univariate extreme value theory

This section is divided according to the two main parts of extreme value theory. First, we will look at models for the largest observations collected from large samples of identically distributed observations, called block maxima models. Then we look at models for all large observations that exceed some high level, called threshold models.

Most of this section is based on the books by Embrechts *et al.* (1997), McNeil *et al.* (2005) and de Haan and Ferreira (2006). The reader may refer to these texts for details.

The generalized extreme value distribution

Our interest is to find possible limit distributions, as the sample size n tends to infinity, for the sample maximum of independent and identically distributed random variables. Let F be the underlying distribution and x_+ its right endpoint, that is $x_+ := \sup\{x : F(x) < 1\}$. Then we have

$$\mathbb{P}(\max(X_1, \ldots, X_n) \leq x) = \mathbb{P}(X_1 \leq x, \ldots, X_n \leq x) = F^n(x), \qquad (2.11)$$

which converges to zero for $x < x_+$ and to 1 for $x \geq x_+$. Hence, we need a normalization in order to obtain a nondegenerate limit distribution as the sample size tends to infinity. In theorem 2.4.1 we see that the only possible nondegenerate limiting distributions for the normalized maxima are in the class of the generalized extreme value (GEV) distribution. Let, for ease of notation, $M_n = \max(X_1, \ldots, X_n)$.

Theorem 2.4.1: Fisher-Tippett Theorem

Suppose that there exists a sequence of constants $a_n > 0$ and $b_n \in \mathbb{R}$ such that

$$\frac{M_n - b_n}{a_n} = \frac{\max(X_1, \ldots, X_n) - b_n}{a_n} \qquad (2.12)$$

has a nondegenerate limit distribution as $n \to \infty$, that is,

$$\lim_{n \to \infty} \mathbb{P}\left(\frac{M_n - b_n}{a_n} \leq x\right) = \lim_{n \to \infty} F^n(a_n x + b_n) = G(x) \qquad (2.13)$$

for a nondegenerate distribution function G. Then G is a member of the GEV family given by

$$G_\gamma(x) = \exp(-(1 + \gamma x)^{-\frac{1}{\gamma}}), \quad 1 + \gamma x > 0, \quad \gamma \in \mathbb{R}. \qquad (2.14)$$

When $\gamma = 0$, the right hand side is interpreted as $\exp(-e^{-x})$.

Proof: See Embrechts *et al.* (1997) or de Haan and Ferreira (2006).

The generalized extreme value distribution is generalized in the sense that it contains three distributions which are known under other names according to the value of γ. Let us consider the three subclasses separately:

1. For $\gamma > 0$ it is a Fréchet distribution. The right endpoint of this distribution is infinity. Moreover, it is classified as a heavy-tailed distribution.
2. For $\gamma = 0$ it is a Gumbel distribution. The right endpoint of this distribution is also infinity. However, the distribution is rather lightly tailed.
3. For $\gamma < 0$ it is a Weibull distribution. The right endpoint of the distribution is $-\frac{1}{\gamma}$, so it has a short tail.

Definition 2.4.2: Maximum domain of attraction

If equation 2.13 holds for some nondegenerate distribution function G_γ, then F is said to be in the maximum domain of attraction of G_γ, written $F \in \text{MDA}(G_\gamma)$.

In de Haan and Ferreira (2006) we find necessary and sufficient conditions on the initial distribution F such that equation 2.13 holds, but, according to McNeil *et al.* (2005), essentially all the common continuous distributions of statistical and actuarial science are in the maximum domain of attraction of G_γ for some value of γ.

The generalized Pareto distribution

In this case we are interested in the distribution of an observation that we know exceeds a given threshold. We have that

$$\mathbb{P}(X > t + x \mid X > t) = \frac{1 - F(t + x)}{1 - F(t)}. \tag{2.15}$$

However, we are interested in the limit distribution when the threshold t and the sample size tends to infinity.

Let X be a random variable with distribution function F and let $F \in \mathrm{MDA}(G_\gamma)$. Then it can be shown that this limit distribution is in the class of the generalized Pareto distribution (GPD). The details can be found in any text book on extreme value theory, for instance, de Haan and Ferreira (2006, page 65).

Definition 2.4.3: Generalizied Pareto distribution

The distribution function of the GPD is given by

$$H_\gamma(x) = 1 - (1 + \gamma x)^{-\frac{1}{\gamma}}, \quad 1 + \gamma x > 0, \quad \gamma \in \mathbb{R}. \tag{2.16}$$

When $\gamma = 0$, the right hand side is interpreted as $1 - e^{-x}$.

Like the GEV the GPD is generalized in the sense that it contains three distributions which are known under other names according to the value of γ. Let us consider these subclasses separately:

1. For $\gamma > 0$ it is a Pareto distribution. The right endpoint of this distribution is infinity. Moreover, it is classified as a heavy-tailed distribution.
2. For $\gamma = 0$ it is the exponential distribution. The right endpoint of this distribution also equals infinity. However, the distribution is rather lightly tailed.
3. For $\gamma < 0$ it is a Pareto type 2 distribution. The right endpoint of the distribution is $-\frac{1}{\gamma}$, so it has a short tail.

Parameter estimation:

Note that the extreme value index γ is the same for the GEV and the GPD. This makes it clear that the estimation of γ is a vital part of extreme value theory. The problem with the estimation stems from the fact that extreme events by nature are rare. Since we naturally do not have many extreme observations, if any, we try to extrapolate into areas which one does not have data. This is also why EVT has been criticised. But still, most people feel that a well founded method based on EVT is better than guesswork. See, for instance, Chavez-Demoulin and Roehrl (2004) for a short and informal motivation of extreme value theory.

For details about methods of estimation of γ, we refer to Embrechts *et al.* (1997) and de Haan and Ferreira (2006).

2.4.2 Multivariate extreme value theory

We have seen that the only possible nondegenerate limiting distributions for the normalized maxima are in the class of generalized extreme value distributions. In multivariate extreme value theory (MEV) this is extended to the multivariate case.

Let $X_1, \ldots, X_n$ be i.i.d. random vectors in $\mathbb{R}^d$ with common multivariate distribution function F and marginal distribution functions $F_1, \ldots, F_d$. One interpretation can be that they represent daily losses over n days for d different risk factors. Let the maximum of the jth component be $M_{n,j} = \max(X_{1,j}, \ldots, X_{n,j})$ for $j = 1, \ldots, d$. We can now define the component block maxima as $M_n = (M_{n,1}, \ldots, M_{n,d})'$.

Note on notation: Note that all arithmetic operations on vectors having equal number of components are done componentvise. Consequently, we let

$$ax + b = (a_1 x_1 + b_1, \ldots, a_d x_d + b_d),$$

and

$$x^k = (x_1^k, \ldots, x_d^k).$$

We are interested in the asymptotic behaviour of M_n. As in the univariate case we need some kind of normalization to reach a nondegenerate limit distribution as the sample size n tends to infinity. Let

$$\frac{M_n - b_n}{a_n} = \left(\frac{M_{n,1} - b_{n,1}}{a_{n,1}}, \ldots, \frac{M_{n,d} - b_{n,d}}{a_{n,d}} \right)', \tag{2.17}$$

where $a_n = (a_{n,1}, \dots, a_{n,d})'$ and $b_n = (b_{n,1}, \dots, b_{n,d})'$ are vectors of normalization constants.

Definition 2.4.4: Multivariate extreme value distribution

Suppose there exists a sequence of constants $a_n > 0$ and $b_n \in \mathbb{R}^d$, such that

$$\frac{M_n - b_n}{a_n} \tag{2.18}$$

has a nondegenerated limit distribution as $n \to \infty$, that is,

$$\lim_{n \to \infty} \mathbb{P}\left(\frac{M_n - b_n}{a_n} \leq x\right) = F^n(a_n x + b_n) = G(x) \tag{2.19}$$

for a nondegenerate distribution function G. Then G is a multivariate extreme value distribution.

Definition 2.4.5: Maximum domain of attraction

If equation 2.19 holds for some nondegenerate distribution function G, then F is said to be in the maximum domain of attraction of G. We write $F \in \mathrm{MDA}(G)$.

If the limiting distribution in equation 2.19 exists, multivariate extreme value theory tells us that each of its univariate margins must be in the family of generalized extreme value distributions. Consequently, the problem of finding the normalization can therefore be done in the univariate setting.

3
Dependence

It is very important to have a good measure of dependence between random variables; we need to know if there is dependence or independence, if the relationship is weak or strong, or if the dependence is varying over the support of the variables. There are a variety of ways to measure and describe dependence between random variables. The most used measures of dependence are the correlation coefficient, Spearman's ρ, Kendall's τ and the tail dependence coefficient. We will shortly introduce these four measures and some of the theory on them. In addition to this we take a brief look at the local dependence function.

We have divided this chapter into two main parts, global and local dependence. Global measures, like linear correlation and rank correlations, are called global because they are constant over the support of the variables. Local dependence measures, on the other hand, allow for a changing dependence over the support of the variables. Consequently, they give us further knowledge about the dependence structure.

We will not give an exhaustive presentation of the theory on local dependence, but we will introduce the tail dependence coefficient and try to apply what we call a dependence map on the return of individual stocks against the a market portfolio. If we can see any pattern in the dependence map, this will give us valuable information on the dependence structure.

For a good review of global and local dependence measures we recommend Hufthammer (2005).

3.1 Global dependence

In this section we will shortly describe global dependence measures like the correlation coefficient and the rank correlations. These measures yield a scalar measure of dependence between a pair of random variables and are therefore called global dependence measures.

3.1.1 The correlation coefficient

Although the word 'correlation' sometimes is used to describe the existence of a general relationship, it should not be confused with the more specific meaning in the context of the correlation coefficient. The correlation coefficient is only a measure of *linear* dependence between two random variables.

Let X_1 and X_2 be two random variables with existing second-order moments. The covariance between X_1 and X_2 is the number defined by

Definition 3.1.1: Covariance

$$\mathrm{Cov}(X_1, X_2) = \mathbb{E}\big[(X_1 - \mathbb{E}\, X_1)(X_2 - \mathbb{E}\, X_2)\big] \tag{3.1}$$
$$= \mathbb{E}(X_1 X_2) - \mathbb{E}(X_1)\,\mathbb{E}(X_2). \tag{3.2}$$

We see that the covariance will be positive when large (small) values of X tends to be observed with large (small) values of Y. If large (small) values of X are associated with small (large) values of Y, the covariance will be negative.

Definition 3.1.2: Correlation

Assuming non-zero but finite variances, the correlation coefficient ρ_{X_1, X_2} is the number defined by

$$\rho_{X_1, X_2} = \frac{\mathrm{Cov}(X_1, X_2)}{\mathrm{SD}(X_1)\,\mathrm{SD}(X_2)}. \tag{3.3}$$

The correlation is unit free and takes values in $[-1,1]$. If the correlation between the random variables X_1 and X_2 is equal to 1 or -1, it implies that $X_1 = a + bX_2$, where a and b are constants, in other words, a perfect linear relationship. If the variables are independent, the correlation is zero. But, if two variables are uncorrelated it does not necessarily imply that they are independent. In addition to this, it can be shown that the attainable correlation can form a strict subset of the interval $[-1,1]$. This tells us that we have to be careful when we state that a small correlation imply a low dependence.

For more details on the properties of the correlation coefficient we again recommend Embrechts *et al.* (2002). They give a review of the shortcomings of the correlation coefficient, and they write about common pitfalls the practitioner must be aware of when dealing with the correlation coefficient as a measure of dependence.

As an illustration of the shortcomings of the correlation coefficient we refer to figure 4.6 on page 52. In this plot, based on an example given in McNeil *et al.* (2005), we have 1,500 simulated observations from four distributions with standard normal margins and equal correlation coefficient $\rho = 0.7$. The marginals are coupled using different 'copulas'. Even though the correlation coefficient and the marginal distributions are *equal* in all four distributions, it is clear that they have *different* dependence structures.

An alternative formulation of the covariance is given by Hoeffding. It is useful for calculating the so called attainable correlation, and it will be used to show that the correlation is not a copula property.

Lemma 3.1.3: Hoeffding's expression of covariance

$$\text{Cov}(X_1, X_2) = \int_{-\infty}^{\infty} \int_{-\infty}^{\infty} \left[F(x_1, x_2) - F_1(x_1) F_2(x_2) \right] dx_1 \, dx_2. \qquad (3.4)$$

Proof: See McNeil *et al.* (2005, page 204).

3.1.2 Rank correlations

Rank correlations are non-parametric dependence measures based on the ranks of the observations. Unlike the usual correlation, where one observation can completely change the estimated value, the estimators of rank correlations are not affected so much by the actual numerical values. This property makes the rank correlations more robust.

Another property of the rank correlations is that they are invariant to strictly increasing transformations. Measures with this property are called scale-invariant. We will see in section 4.8 on page 61 that scale-invariant properties of the distribution function actually are properties of the corresponding copula. Since the rank correlations are functions of the copula only, they can be used to estimate the parameters of the copula. This will be further described in chapter 5.

Below we investigate two of the most used rank correlations coefficients, namely Kendall's τ and Spearman's ρ. Both measure a form of dependence known as concordance.

Concordance

A pair of random variables is said to be concordant if large (small) values of one variable tend to occur with large (small) values of the other.

Definition 3.1.4: Concordance and discordance

We say that two observations (x_1, x_2) and $(\tilde{x}_1, \tilde{x}_2)$ from a random vector (X_1, X_2) are *concordant* if and only if

$$q = (x_1 - \tilde{x}_1)(x_2 - \tilde{x}_2) > 0. \tag{3.5}$$

If the inequality is changed to strictly *less* than, we say that the variables are *discordant*. This is illustrated in figure 3.1.

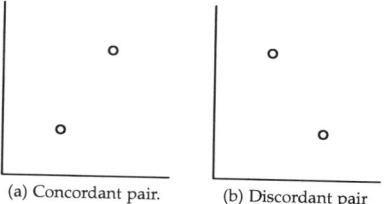

(a) Concordant pair.   (b) Discordant pair

Figure 3.1: Figure (a) shows a concordant pair and figure (b) shows a discordant pair.

Kendall's τ and Spearman's ρ are examples of true concordance measures. The properties a measure of concordance should satisfy, and the fact that

Kendall's τ and Spearman's ρ are true measures of concordance, can be found in Nelsen (2006, page 169). Note that the linear correlation coefficient in general do not satisfy the properties of a concordance measure.

Kendall's τ

Definition 3.1.5: Kendall's τ

Consider two independent random vectors (X_1, X_2) and $(\tilde{X}_1, \tilde{X}_2)$ with the same bivariate distribution. Kendall's τ is defined as the probability of concordance minus the probability of discordance.

$$\tau(X_1, X_2) = \mathbb{P}((X_1 - \tilde{X}_1)(X_2 - \tilde{X}_2) > 0) \tag{3.6}$$
$$- \mathbb{P}((X_1 - \tilde{X}_1)(X_2 - \tilde{X}_2) < 0). \tag{3.7}$$

If X_1 tends to increase with X_2, we expect the probability of concordance to be relatively high compared to the probability of discordance.

The sample estimate of Kendall's τ is quite intuitive. If we have n independent observations $(x_{11}, x_{21}), \ldots, (x_{1n}, x_{2n})$ of a bivariate random vector (X_1, X_2), Kendall's τ is usually estimated by

$$\hat{\tau} = \frac{\text{number of concordant pairs} - \text{number of discordante pairs}}{\text{number of pairs}}, \tag{3.8}$$

which can be written as

$$\binom{n}{2}^{-1} \sum_{i<j} \text{sign}\left[(x_{1i} - x_{1j})(x_{2i} - x_{2j})\right], \tag{3.9}$$

where $\text{sign}(x)$ is the usual signum function.

As with the linear correlation we can give an alternative definition of Kendall's τ. This will be used in section 4.8 on page 61 to show that Kendall's τ is a property of the copula alone.

Lemma 3.1.6: Alternative expression of Kendall's τ

$$\tau(X_1, X_2) = 4 \int_{-\infty}^{\infty} \int_{-\infty}^{\infty} F(x_1, x_2) \, dF(x_1, x_2) - 1. \tag{3.10}$$

Proof: See McNeil *et al.* (2005, page 207).

Spearman's ρ

Spearman's ρ can also be defined in terms of concordance and discordance, but for our purpose we define it in a more intuitive way. If X_1 and X_2 are continuous variables with distribution functions F_1 and F_2, then $U_1 = F_1(X_1)$ and $U_2 = F_2(X_2)$ are uniformly distributed on $\mathbb{I} = [0,1]$. Spearman's rank correlation is defined as the correlation between U_1 and U_2:

Definition 3.1.7: Spearman's ρ

$$\rho_s(X_1, X_2) = \operatorname{corr}(F_1(X_1), F_2(X_2)) = \operatorname{corr}(U_1, U_2) \qquad (3.11)$$

$$= \frac{\mathbb{E}(U_1 U_2) - \mathbb{E}(U_1)\,\mathbb{E}(U_2)}{\operatorname{SD}(U_1)\,\operatorname{SD}(U_2)} \qquad (3.12)$$

$$= \frac{\mathbb{E}(U_1 U_2) - \frac{1}{4}}{\frac{1}{12}} \qquad (3.13)$$

$$= 12\,\mathbb{E}(U_1 U_2) - 3. \qquad (3.14)$$

Spearman's ρ is calculated by replacing each value by its rank i, and then calculate the usual sample correlation on these ranks.

As we have seen with the linear correlation and Kendall's τ it is possible to give an alternative expression of Spearman's ρ:

Lemma 3.1.8: Alternative expression of Spearman's ρ

$$\rho_s(X_1, X_2) = 12 \int_{-\infty}^{\infty} \int_{-\infty}^{\infty} [F(x_1, x_2) - F_1(x_1)F_2(x_2)]\,dF_1(x_1)\,dF_2(x_2), \quad (3.15)$$

Proof: See McNeil *et al.* (2005, pages 207–208).

This expression will be used in section 4.8 on page 61 to show that Spearman's ρ is a property of the copula alone.

Example 3.1.9: Estimating the correlations

In this example we have estimated Spearman's ρ, Kendall's τ and the linear correlation coefficient on almost 14 years (January 1990 to March 2004) of daily log-returns from three financial indices, the Swiss Market Index (SMI), Standard & Poor 500 (SP) and FTSE500 (FTSE). The results are to be found in table 3.1 on the next page.

These data and the results will be considered further in chapter 5 where it will be used to calibrate parameters for specific copulas.

	FTSE	SMI	SP
FTSE	1.00	0.67	0.40
SMI	0.67	1.00	0.34
SP	0.40	0.34	1.00

(a) Spearman's ρ

	FTSE	SMI	SP
FTSE	1.00	0.49	0.28
SMI	0.49	1.00	0.23
SP	0.28	0.23	1.00

(b) Kendall's τ

	FTSE	SMI	SP
FTSE	1.00	0.72	0.43
SMI	0.72	1.00	0.40
SP	0.43	0.40	1.00

(c) Linear correlation

Table 3.1: Estimated values of Kendall's τ, Spearman's ρ and linear correlation on three indices. See example 3.1.9 on the preceding page for details.

3.2 Local dependence

Sometimes global measures of dependence do not contain enough information on the nature of association. One example is when X_1 is a random variable (with zero mean and third moment) and $X_2 = X_1^2$. In this case we have complete association between X_1 and X_2 but the correlation will be zero. This happens because the strong negative association for $X_1 < 0$ and the strong positive association for $X_1 > 0$ 'cancel each other out'.

Situations like this is hard to imagine in finance, but we sometimes hear people say that 'the correlation increase during financial crisis', or that 'the β (from CAPM) jumps to a larger value at times when the market dives'. This implies that the dependence may vary over the support of the variables. This is reasonable. When the absolute value of the return from the market is *high*, it gives a strong signal of the expectations of the future, and the dependence between an individual stock and the market will be *high*. Similarly we may expect that the dependence is *weak* when the change in the market is *low*. This kind of dependence cannot be captured with a global measure of dependence; we need a local dependence measure.

3.2.1 The local dependence function

The local dependence function is described in Holland and Wang (1987). It is a function of the two variables and its values are hard to interpret. But Jones and Koch (2003) suggested to use a graphical display which they called a dependence map. In this map they used three colours to represent negative dependence, positive dependence and independence.

The dependence map which we use has been improved by Hufthammer (2005) who used a palette of colours to indicate a varying level of local dependence. At each grid point, a colour representation of the value of the local dependence function is shown. The colours are chosen so that it is easy to see if the local dependence is positive or negative, and to compare the strength of the dependence in various areas. This can give us valuable information about the dependence structure.

In figure 3.2 on the facing page to figure 3.4 on page 31 we see dependence maps constructed on daily returns from three individual stocks against the market portfolio. The data are described further in section 2.2.1 on page 9. The basic idea is that these plots could indicate how the strength of the dependence vary over the support of the variables.

From our dependence maps we see that there is a tendency for increasing dependence when the value of the return from the market increase. But for our stocks we do not find the same tendency for negative returns. Since the market has experienced an increasing dependence in negative returns we conclude that it seems reasonable to assume that we have a symmetric but increasing dependence structure between individual stocks and the market. As will be seen, this supports the use of the t-copula (to be defined in equation 4.19) to model return series from stocks.

In addition to this we have produced dependence maps on simulated values from different distributions constructed by using various bivariate copulas (figure 4.13 on page 70 to figure 4.15 on page 72). By simply comparing the dependence maps on the observed stock returns to the dependence maps on the simulated values we conclude that it seems reasonable to use the t-copula to model stock returns.

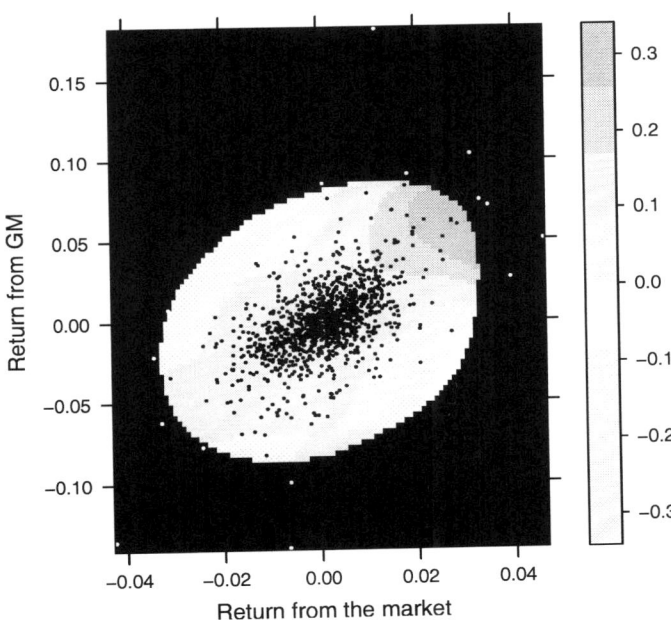

Figure 3.2: A dependence map of the daily returns from General Motors against the daily returns from a market portfolio consisting of three indices: NYSE, FTSE and NASDAQ. We can see that there is a tendency for increased dependence as the value of the return increases.

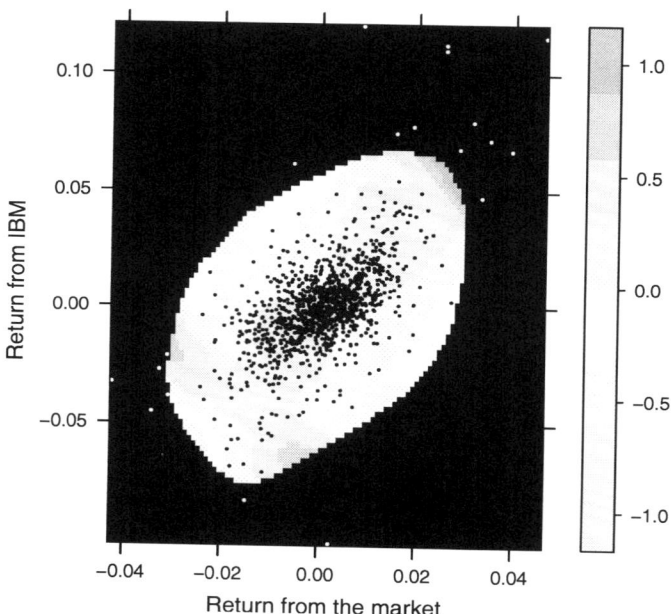

Figure 3.3: A dependence map of the daily returns from IBM against the daily returns from a market portfolio consisting of three indices: NYSE, FTSE and NASDAQ. We can see that there is a tendency for increased dependence as the value of the return increases.

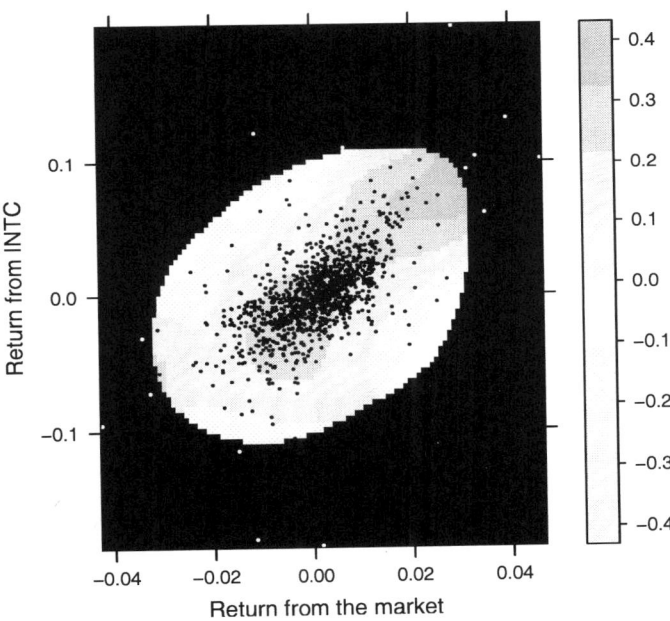

Figure 3.4: A dependence map of the daily return from Intel Corporation INTC
against the daily return from a market portfolio consisting of three
indices: NYSE, FTSE and NASDAQ. We can see that there is a tendency
for increased dependence as the value of the return increases.

3.2.2 Tail dependence

The tail dependence measures the amount of dependence in the upper and lower tail of a bivariate distribution. In the case of upper tail dependence we look at the probability that X_2 exceeds its q-quantile, given that X_1 exceeds its q-quantile, and then consider the limit when q tends to infinity. In other words, the tail dependence coefficient can be consider as the probability that X_1 will be 'large' given that X_2 is 'large'.

It is easy to see why it is important to have a understanding of tail dependence. For instance, the total risk of a portfolio is definitely affected by the presence or absence of tail dependence. If extreme losses appear to occur simultaneously, the total risk is higher than if extreme losses occur independently. Judging the dependence maps in figure 3.2 on page 29 to figure 3.4 on the preceding page it is reasonable to assume that there are some tail dependence present in stock returns.

Definition 3.2.1: Tail dependence

Let $X_1 \sim F_1$ and $X_2 \sim F_2$. Then, by definition, the upper tail dependence coefficient is,

$$\lambda_u(x_1, x_2) = \lim_{q \to 1} \mathbb{P}(X_1 > F_1^{\leftarrow}(q) \mid X_2 > F_2^{\leftarrow}(q)) \qquad (3.16)$$

and analogously for the lower tail dependence,

$$\lambda_l(x_1, x_2) = \lim_{q \to 0} \mathbb{P}(X_1 \leq F_1^{\leftarrow}(q) \mid X_2 \leq F_2^{\leftarrow}(q)). \qquad (3.17)$$

If λ_u or λ_l are in $(0, 1]$, then X_1 and X_2 are said to be asymptotically dependent in the upper or lower tail. If λ_u or λ_l equals 0, they are said to be asymptotically independent in the upper or lower tail.

In section 4.8.2 on page 65 we will see that the tail dependence is a copula property. That is, if (X_1, X_2) are continuous, we can express λ_u and λ_l in terms of the copula of (X_1, X_2) only. As a direct consequence of this the tail dependence coefficients are independent of the choice of marginals. This will be treated in more details in section 4.8.2 on page 65 where we, among other things, calculate the tail dependence coefficients for various distributions.

See Frahm *et al.* (2005) for a note on the estimation of the tail dependence coefficient.

4

Copulas

In chapter 2 we saw that the joint distribution function contains all the information about the marginal distributions (equation 2.2 on page 4). Indeed, it is well known that by using elliptical distributions we force the marginals to be in the *same* class of univariate distributions[1]. This is not satisfactory when we work with variables with different properties, as when we model the portfolio of a financial institution. This motivates an investigation of the copulas. In a copula model the only restriction is that the marginals should be continuous.

Since the multivariate distribution completely determine the marginal distributions, while on the other hand, the marginal distributions do *not* determine the joint distributions, it is clear that joint distributions contain more information than marginals. Sklar (1959) showed that this additional information can be captured in a dependence function which he called the copula. The essence of Sklar's theorem (to be given in theorem 4.2.1 on page 39) is that we can split a joint distribution into two parts: the copula, which describes the dependence, and the marginal distributions. Moreover, Sklar's theorem states that if we know the marginal distributions and the copula, then we actually know the multivariate distribution.

---

[1]The marginals of an elliptical distribution are themself elliptical and have the same characteristic function (See, for instance, Lindskog *et al.* (2003); McNeil *et al.* (2005)).

This gives us a great flexibility. We have a procedure to create multivariate distributions with arbitrary marginal distributions; we do not have any restrictions on the marginals other than that they should be continuous, and we have a rich set of copulas to describe the dependence.

In section 4.1 we give a mathematical introduction, where we describe the properties a function must satisfy in order to be a copula, and in section 4.2 on page 38 we introduce Sklar's theorem. Sklar's theorem is probably the most important theorem in relation to copulas and it explains why copulas have become popular in statistics. After this we continue this chapter by giving examples of the most common copulas, and we describe their properties in some detail.

4.1 Mathematical introduction

It is common to define the copulas in a probabilistic way. We usually say that a copula is a 'function that joins, or couple, multivariate distribution functions to their marginal distribution functions', or that a copula is a 'distribution functions whose one-dimensional marginals are uniform'. This is a natural working definition, but it does not say anything about the properties a function should have in order to be a copula. In this section we first describe the properties a function must satisfy in order to be a multivariate distribution, and then we use this to give a proper definition of the copula. This section is based on Nelsen (2006) and Embrechts *et al.* (2001), and the reader may refer to these texts when details are missing and proofs are omitted.

Let us first define some notation. For a function H we denote by $\mathrm{Dom}\,H$ and $\mathrm{Ran}\,H$ the domain and the range of H, respectively. We let $\mathbb{R}$ denote the real line $(-\infty, \infty)$, $\overline{\mathbb{R}}$ the extended real line $[-\infty, \infty]$, and $\overline{\mathbb{R}}^d$ the extended d-space $\overline{\mathbb{R}} \times \cdots \times \overline{\mathbb{R}}$. With a real-valued function in d variables we will mean a function whose domain is a subset of $\overline{\mathbb{R}}^d$ and whose range is a subset of $\mathbb{R}$. We use a vector notation for points in $\overline{\mathbb{R}}^d$, for example $\boldsymbol{a} = (a_1, \ldots, a_d)$. The notation $\boldsymbol{a} \le \boldsymbol{b}$ will mean that $a_k \le b_k$, for all k.

For $\boldsymbol{a} \le \boldsymbol{b}$, we will let $[\boldsymbol{a}, \boldsymbol{b}] = [a_1, b_1] \times [a_2, b_2] \times \cdots \times [a_d, b_d]$ denote the d-box. The vertices of an d-box are the points $\boldsymbol{c} = (c_1, \ldots c_d)$ where c_k is equal to either a_k or b_k. Note that a 2-box is a rectangle $[x_1, x_2] \times [y_1, y_2]$ in $\overline{\mathbb{R}}^2$, and in this case the vertices of the 2-box are the points $(x_1, y_1), (x_1, y_2), (x_2, y_1)$ and (x_2, y_2), that is, the corners of the rectangle.

Definition 4.1.1: *H*-volume

Let $S_1, \ldots, S_d$ be nonempty subsets of $\overline{\mathbb{R}}$. Let H be a real-valued function in d variables such that $\text{Dom } H = S_1 \times \cdots \times S_d$. For $a \leq b$, let $B = [a, b]$ be a d-box whose vertices are in $\text{Dom } H$. The H-volume of B is then defined to be

$$V_H(B) = \sum \text{sign}(c) H(c), \tag{4.1}$$

where the sum is taken over all vertices c of B, and $\text{sign}(c)$ is

$$\text{sign}(c) = \begin{cases} 1, & \text{if } c_k = a_k \text{ for an even number of } k; \\ -1, & \text{if } c_k = a_k \text{ for an odd number of } k. \end{cases} \tag{4.2}$$

Example 4.1.2: *H*-volume

The H-volume of the 2-box $B = [x_1, x_1] \times [y_1, y_2]$ is

$$V_H(B) = H(x_2, y_2) - H(x_1, y_2) - H(x_2, y_1) + H(x_1, y_1).$$

As we can see, if (X, Y) is a random vector and H is the distribution function, then $V_H(B) = \mathbb{P}(B)$.

With the example above in mind, the concept of d-increasing functions is very natural in the context of distribution functions. The definition is as follows.

Definition 4.1.3: *d*-increasing functions

A real-valued function H is d-increasing if $V_H(B) \geq 0$ for all d-boxes B whose vertices lie in $\text{Dom } H$.

From this we see that a distribution function has to be d-increasing.

The definitions of grounded functions and marginals are also very natural in the context of a distribution function.

Definition 4.1.4: Margins and grounded functions

Suppose that the domain of a real-valued function H of d variables is given by $\text{Dom } H = S_1 \times \cdots \times S_d$, where each S_k has a least element a_k. We say that H is grounded if $H(t) = 0$ for all t in $\text{Dom } H$ such that $t_k = a_k$ for at least one k.

If in addition, each S_k has a greatest element, say b_k, the margins of H are the functions H_k with $\text{Dom } H_k = S_k$ and

$$H_k(x) = H(b_1, \ldots, b_{k-1}, x, b_{k+1}, \ldots, b_d), \quad \text{for } x \text{ in } S_k.$$

Higher dimensional margins are defined by fixing fewer places in H and are called k-margins for $2 \le k \le d - 1$.

In addition to this, a distribution function should be nondecreasing in each argument. Recall that the function H is nondecreasing in each argument if $H(t_1, \ldots, x, \ldots, t_d) \le H(t_1, \ldots, y, \ldots, t_d)$ for all $x \le y$ with t_k's in $\text{Dom } H$. This leads us to the following lemma which basically states that a grounded d-increasing function is nondecreasing in each argument.

Lemma 4.1.5: Nondecreasing in each argument

If $S_1, \ldots, S_d$ are nonempty subsets of $\overline{\mathbb{R}}^d$ and H is a grounded d-increasing function with domain $S_1 \times \cdots \times S_d$, then H is nondecreasing in each argument.

The next lemma will be used to show that copulas are uniformly continuous.

Lemma 4.1.6

If $S_1, \ldots, S_d$ are nonempty subsets of $\overline{\mathbb{R}}^d$ and H is a grounded d-increasing function with domain $S_1 \times \cdots \times S_d$, then, for points x and y in $\text{Dom}(H)$,

$$|H(x) - H(y)| \le \sum_{k=1}^{d} |H_k(x_k) - H_k(y_k)|. \tag{4.3}$$

Proof: This follows from the fact that the function H is grounded, d-increasing and has margins. For a proof for 2-increasing functions, see (Nelsen 2006, page 9); see Schweizer and Sklar (1983) for a proof in the general case.

Using these definitions we are able to define the d-dimensional distribution function in an alternative way.

Definition 4.1.7: Distribution functions

An d-dimensional distribution function is a function H with domain $\overline{\mathbb{R}}^d$ such that H is grounded, d-increasing and $H(\infty, \ldots, \infty) = 1$.

This definition is different from the one we usually see in probability theory, but we are now in a position to define the copulas in a more formal way than the standard operational definition.

Definition 4.1.8: Copulas

An d-dimensional copula is a function C with domain $\mathbb{I}^d = [0,1]^n$ with the following properties:

1. C is grounded.
2. C is d-increasing.
3. C has margins C_k, for $k = 1, \ldots, d$ that satisfy $C_k(u) = u$ for all u in $\mathbb{I} = [0,1]$.

Or we can state the following alternative, but equivalent, definition.

Definition 4.1.9: Alternative definition of a copula

A d-dimensional copula is a function C from $\mathbb{I}^d$ to $\mathbb{I}$ with the following properties:

1. For every u in $\mathbb{I}^d$

$$C(u) = 0 \text{ if at least one coordinate of } u \text{ is } 0, \text{ and} \qquad (4.4)$$
$$C(u) = u_k \text{ if all coordinate of } u \text{ except } u_k \text{ are } 1. \qquad (4.5)$$

2. For every a and b in $\mathbb{I}^d$ such that $a \le b$,

$$V_C([a,b]) \ge 0. \qquad (4.6)$$

From lemma 4.1.6 on the preceding page it follows directly that copulas are uniformly continuous on $[0,1]^d$.

Theorem 4.1.10: Uniformly continuous

Let C be a d-copula. Then for every u and v in $[0,1]^d$,

$$|C(v) - C(u)| \le \sum_{k=1}^{d} |v_k - u_k|. \qquad (4.7)$$

Subcopulas

Since this thesis focus on the role of copulas in statistics we have so far not mentioned subcopulas. But since many of the the properties of copulas actually are properties of subcopulas, and since it is common to define copulas in terms of subcopulas, we will introduce them. As we can see in the following definitions, a subcopula is a function with the same properties as a copula, but with a different domain. Every copula is a subcopula, but not every subcopula is a copula.

Definition 4.1.11: Subcopulas

An d-dimensional subcopula is a function C' with the following properties:

1. $\text{Dom}\, C' = S_1 \times \cdots \times S_d$, where each S_k is a subset of $\mathbb{I}$ containing 0 and 1.
2. C' is grounded.
3. C' is d-increasing.
4. C' has margins C_k, for $k = 1, \ldots, d$ that satisfy $C_k(u) = u$ for all u in S_k.

We are now in the position to give a third definition of a copula.

Definition 4.1.12: Alternative definition copulas

An d-dimensional copula is a d-subcopula whose domain is $\mathbb{I}^d$.

4.2 A probabilistic setting

It is clear from the above definitions that a copula is a multivariate distribution with support in $[0,1]^d$ and uniform marginals. From the definition of the copula, and since the random variable $F_i(X_i) \sim U(0,1)$, we obtain

$$F(x_1, \ldots, x_d) = \mathbb{P}(F_1(X_1) \le F_1(x_1), \ldots, F_d(X_d) \le F_d(x_d)) \qquad (4.8)$$
$$= C(F_1(x_1), \ldots, F_d(x_d)). \qquad (4.9)$$

We see that we can separate the multivariate distribution into two parts: the copula, which describes the dependence, and the marginals $F_1 \ldots, F_d$.

Sklar's theorem says that equation 4.9 holds in general: joint distribution functions can be written in terms of the marginals and a (not necessarily unique) copula. The word copula was chosen carefully by Sklar in his paper from 1959; it is Latin and means a link, bond or tie.

Theorem 4.2.1: Sklar's theorem (1959)

Let F be a joint distribution function with margins $F_1, \ldots, F_d$. Then there exists a copula C such that, for all x in $\overline{\mathbb{R}}^d = [-\infty, \infty]^d$,

$$F(x_1, \ldots, x_d) = C(F_1(x_1), \ldots, F_d(x_d)). \tag{4.10}$$

If the margins are continuous, then C is unique. Otherwise C is uniquely determined on $\text{Ran} F_1 \times \cdots \times \text{Ran} F_d$.

Conversely, for any univariate distribution functions $F_1, \ldots, F_d$ and any copula C, the function $C(F_1, \ldots, F_d)$ is a d-dimensional distribution function with marginals $F_1, \ldots, F_d$. If $F_1, \ldots, F_d$ are continuous, then C is unique.

Proof: Sklar's theorem was given by Sklar (1959). It is in French and no proofs where given. See Schweizer and Sklar (1983) or Nelsen (2006) for proofs.

One important property of the copulas is that they are invariant under strictly increasing transformations, and they change in a predictable way under other monotone transformations (see Nelsen 2006, page 26).

Theorem 4.2.2: Invariant under strictly increasing transformations

Let $X = (X_1, \ldots, X_d)'$ be a random vector with continuous marginal distributions $F_{X_1}, \ldots, F_{X_d}$, joint distribution F_X and copula C. Let $(a_1, \ldots, a_d)$ be strictly increasing functions, then $Z = (a_1(X_1), \ldots, a_d(X_d))$ also has copula C.

4.2.1 Meta distributions

If U has distribution function C, we can transform the data into realizations of X by using the quantile transformation: $X = (F_1^{\leftarrow}(U_1), \ldots, F_d^{\leftarrow}(U_d))'$, where the distribution functions are arbitrary. A distribution with a given copula but arbitrary margins is often referred to as a meta distribution. In this thesis we will look at several examples of meta distributions with standard normal margins. Note that we could have used any other distribution, or a mixture of distributions, but, with odd combinations of the margins, the shape of the scatterplots do not look very useful.

4.3 Implicit copulas

It follows from Sklar's theorem that a copula can be constructed from a joint distribution. Copulas derived from known distributions are called implicit copulas. If the copulas in addition are derived from elliptical distributions, they are often referred to as elliptical copulas. Examples of common elliptical copulas are the normal- and the t-copula, but it is possible to extract the copula of any joint distribution function F with continuous margins. When we have extracted the copula, we can construct new multivariate distributions with arbitrary margins. As mentioned, distributions with arbitrary margins are called meta-distributions.

Lemma 4.3.1: Implicit copulas

We will now consider a multivariate distribution F with continuous marginals $F_1, \ldots, F_d$. Let $u_1, \ldots, u_d$ denote the values of $F_1, \ldots, F_d$. Then the function

$$F(x_1, \ldots, x_d) = \mathbb{P}(F_1(X_1) \leq u_1, \ldots, F_d(X_d) \leq u_d) \quad (4.11)$$
$$= F(F_1^{\leftarrow}(u_1), \ldots, F_d^{\leftarrow}(u_d)) \quad (4.12)$$
$$(4.13)$$

is a d-copula.

We see that the copula of F, where F is defined as above, is the distribution function of the marginals $F_1, \ldots, F_d$.

The Gaussian copula

If Y has a normal distribution $Y \sim N_d(\boldsymbol{\mu}, \boldsymbol{\Sigma})$, then the copula belonging to Y is the Gaussian copula. Since the copula is invariant under strictly increasing transformations, the standardization of the marginals do not affect the copula. The copula of Y is therefore the same as the copula of $X \sim N_d(0, \boldsymbol{R})$, where $\boldsymbol{R}$ is the correlation matrix of Y. The Gaussian copula is given by

$$C_{\boldsymbol{R}}^{\text{GA}}(\boldsymbol{u}) = \mathbb{P}(\Phi(X_1) \leq u_1, \ldots, \Phi(X_d) \leq u_d) \quad (4.14)$$
$$= \boldsymbol{\Phi_R}(\Phi^{-1}(u_1), \ldots, \Phi^{-1}(u_d)), \quad (4.15)$$

where Φ_R denotes the joint distribution of X, Φ is the standard normal distribution function and Φ^{-1} is the usual inverse.

We can now use this copula to create other distributions by changing the marginals. For any given continuous marginals $F_{Z_1}, \ldots, F_{Z_d}$ we get that

$$C_R^{\text{GA}}(u) = \Phi_R\left(\Phi^{-1}(F_{Z_1}(z_1)), \ldots, \Phi^{-1}(F_{Z_d}(z_d))\right) \qquad (4.16)$$

is a distribution function. We see that if $F_{Z_1}, \ldots, F_{Z_d}$ are standard normal the Gaussian copula will generate the usual multivariate normal distribution.

$$C_R^{\text{GA}}(u) = \Phi_R(x_1, \ldots, x_d). \qquad (4.17)$$

In figure 4.1 on the next page we see scatterplots of the bivariate Gaussian copula with $\rho = 0.7$ and the corresponding meta-distributions. The meta-distributions are constructed from the Gaussian copula data by using the quantile function of the standard normal, the standard t, and the exponential distribution with $\lambda = 1$, respectively.

From equation A.8 on page 103 we see that the density of the Gaussian copula is given by

$$c_R^{\text{GA}}(u) = \frac{f_R(\Phi_1^{-1}(u_1), \ldots, \Phi_d^{-1}(u_d))}{\prod_{i=1}^d f(\Phi^{-1}(u_i))}, \qquad (4.18)$$

where f_R is the joint density of $X \sim N_d(0, R)$ and f is the univariate density of the standard normal distribution.

The t-copula

It is possible to extract the copula of any multivariate distribution function with continuous margins. As in the case of the normal distribution, the standardization of the marginals do not affect the copula. Consequently, the copula of the multivariate t-distribution $t_d(\mu, \Sigma, \nu)$ (section 2.3.1) is identical to the copula of the standardized multivariate t-distribution $t_d(0, R, \nu)$. We can therefore extract the copula of the t-distribution in the same way as for the normal distribution.

$$C_{\nu, R}^{\text{T}} = t_{\nu, R}(t_\nu^{-1}(u_1), \ldots, t_\nu^{-1}(u_d)), \qquad (4.19)$$

where $t_{\nu, R}$ is the distribution of $X \sim t_d(0, R, \nu)$ and t_ν is the univariate distribution function of the standard t-distribution. Note that for $\nu > 2$, R is the·

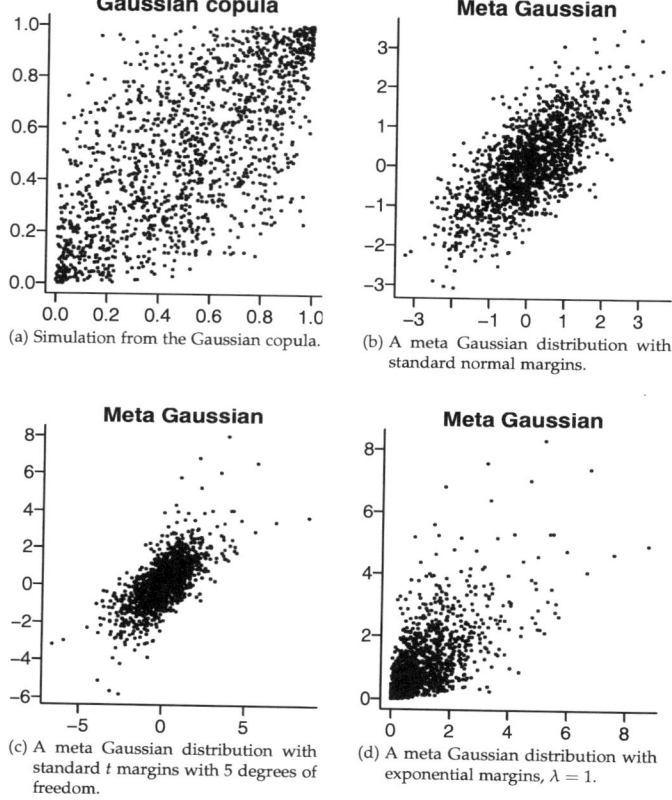

(a) Simulation from the Gaussian copula.

(b) A meta Gaussian distribution with standard normal margins.

(c) A meta Gaussian distribution with standard t margins with 5 degrees of freedom.

(d) A meta Gaussian distribution with exponential margins, $\lambda = 1$.

Figure 4.1: Figure (a) shows a scatterplot of 1,500 simulated points from the bivariate Gaussian copula with $\rho = 0.7$. In figure (b) we have transformed the data with the quantile function of the standard normal distribution. Consequently, it is a scatterplot of the usual bivariate normal distribution. In figure (c) and (d) we have transformed the Gaussian copula data by using the quantile function of the t-distribution and the exponential distribution, respectively.

usual linear correlation coefficient implied by the dispersion matrix Σ (see section 2.3.1 on page 13.).

We have argued that the dependence between stocks are high when the absolute value of the returns are high; in other words, that there is a symmetric dependence structure between the stocks and the market. This kind of symmetric dependence is captured by the t-copula, and this makes this copula very interesting when modelling multivariate financial return data.

Moreover, we have seen that there are some evidence that the univariate distribution of the monthly returns follow a normal distribution, but the multivariate normality assumption is rejected. We concluded that this is probably because the multivariate normal distribution do not assign enough weight to joint extreme observations. This motivates the use of the t-copula with normal margins to model monthly returns from stocks.

The Cauchy copula is a special case of the t-copulas where the degrees of freedom $\nu = 1$.

From equation A.8 on page 103 we see that the density of the t-copula is given by

$$c_{\nu,R}^{T}(u) = \frac{f_{\nu,R}(t_\nu^{-1}(u_1), \ldots, t_\nu^{-1}(u_d))}{\prod_{i=1}^{d} f_\nu(t_\nu^{-1}(u_i))}, \tag{4.20}$$

where $f_{\nu,R}$ is the joint density of $X \sim t_d(0, R, \nu)$ and f_ν is the univariate density of the standard t-distribution.

In figure 4.2a on the next page we see a scatterplot of simulated values from the bivariate t-copula with $\rho = 0.7$, and in figure 4.2b on the following page we have transformed the data using the quantile function of the standard normal distribution. We see that the dependence tends to increase in the upper and lower tail.

For futher details about the t-copula, see Demarta and McNeil (2005).

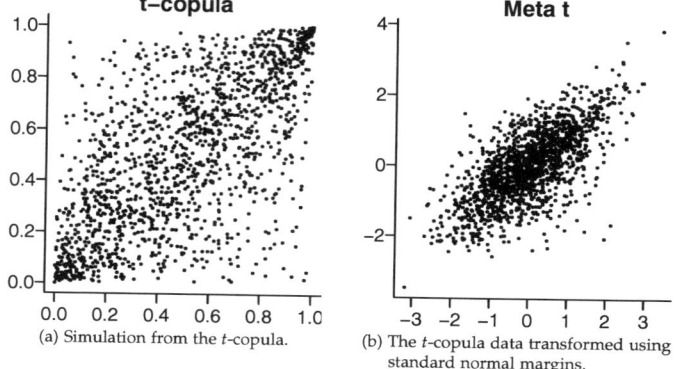

(a) Simulation from the *t*-copula.

(b) The *t*-copula data transformed using standard normal margins.

Figure 4.2: Figure (a) shows a scatterplot of 1,500 simulated points from the bivariate *t*-copula with $\rho = 0.7$ and 4 degrees of freedom. In figure (b) we have transformed the data with the quantile function of the standard normal distribution.

4.4 Archimedean copulas

We have tried to argue that possibly dependence between stocks are higher when the losses or the gains are 'high', but one can also argue that the dependence increases during periods of distress, in other words, that there is a stronger relationship between big losses than between big gains. In situations like this we the need asymmetric copulas and these can be found in the class of Archimedean copulas. The Archimedean copulas have been much studied, and are usefull for several reasons.

1. They are easy to construct.
2. There are a great variety of copulas belonging to this class.
3. They have a closed form expression.
4. They are not restricted to have radial symmetry (definition A.2.3 on page 102).

But Archimedean copulas also have some disadvantages, especially when the dimension is larger than two. In the Gaussian and the *t*-copula we can assign pairwise dependence by the correlation matrix. The Archimedean copulas, on the other hand, are generally not rich in parameters, and this limits the nature of dependence relations they can model. This is a drawback, but Archimedean copulas can still be suitable for small homogeneous random vectors, that is, vectors where it is reasonable to have equal dependence between the variables.

As a motivation we start by an obvious example of an Archimedean copula, namely the independence copula. If $X = (X_1, \ldots, X_d)'$ are independent random variables, then we have that

$$F_X(x) = \prod_{i=1}^{d} F_i(x_i). \tag{4.21}$$

This can immediately be rewritten in the form

$$F_X(x) = \exp(-[(-\ln F_1(x_1)) + \cdots + (-\ln F_d(x_d))]) \tag{4.22}$$
$$= \varphi^{-1}(\varphi(F_1(x_1)) + \cdots + \varphi(F_d(x_d))), \tag{4.23}$$

where $\varphi(t) = -\ln(t)$ is known as the generator function.

It turns out that this trivial result can be generalized to sequences of dependent random variables (see Kimberling 1974), and copulas with the form of equation 4.23 will be called Archimedean copulas. These copulas are completely defined by their generator function φ. To define Archimedean copulas we have to define the properties the generator function φ must satisfy in order to generate copulas.

The following section is based on the work by Nelsen (2006), Embrechts *et al.* (2001) and McNeil *et al.* (2005), further details can be found in these texts.

Bivariate Archimedean copulas

As indicated, a bivariate Archimedean copula is on the form

$$C(u_1, u_2) = \varphi^{-1}(\varphi(u_1) + \varphi(u_2)), \tag{4.24}$$

where φ^{-1} is the usual inverse and φ is a continuous, strictly decreasing, convex function $\varphi : [0, 1] \to [0, \infty]$ satisfying $\varphi(1) = 0$. But since $\varphi(u_1) + \varphi(u_2)$ can be outside the domain of φ^{-1} we need to introduce the pseudo-inverse.

Definition 4.4.1: The pseudo-inverse of the generator function

Let φ be a continuous, strictly decreasing function from $[0, 1]$ to $[0, \infty]$ such that $\varphi(1) = 0$. The pseudo-inverse of φ is the function $\varphi^{[-1]} : [0, \infty] \to [0, 1]$

given by

$$\varphi^{[-1]}(t) = \begin{cases} \varphi^{-1}(t), & 0 \leq t \leq \varphi(0), \\ 0, & \varphi(0) \leq t \leq \infty. \end{cases} \tag{4.25}$$

Note that if $\varphi(0) = \infty$, then $\varphi^{[-1]} = \varphi^{-1}$.

See example 4.4.7 on page 50 for an example where we need this definition.

We are now able to give a formal definition of the bivariate Archimedean copula.

Theorem 4.4.2: Bivariate Archimedean copula

A bivariate Archimedean copula is a copula on the form

$$C(u_1, u_2) = \varphi^{[-1]}(\varphi(u_1) + \varphi(u_2)), \tag{4.26}$$

where the generator function φ is a strictly decreasing function from $[0, 1]$ to $[0, \infty]$, where $\varphi(1) = 0$ and $\varphi^{[-1]}$ is its pseudo-inverse.

Theorem 4.4.3: Construction of Archimedean copulas

Let φ be a strictly decreasing function from $[0, 1]$ to $[0, \infty]$ such that $\varphi(1) = 0$. Then

$$C(u_1, u_2) = \varphi^{[-1]}(\varphi(u_1) + \varphi(u_2)) \tag{4.27}$$

is a copula if and only if φ is convex.

Proof: See Nelsen (2006, pages 111–112).

We end this by formally defining the generator function and the strict generator function.

Definition 4.4.4: The generator function and strict Archimedean copulas

A continuous, strictly decreasing, convex function $\varphi : [0, 1] \rightarrow [0, \infty]$ satisfying $\varphi(1) = 0$ is known as an Archimedean copula generator. It is a *strict* generator if $\varphi(0) = \infty$, where it is common to write $\varphi(0) = \infty$ if $\lim_{t \to 0} \varphi(t) = \infty$. Archimedean copulas with a strict generator function are referred to as strict Archimedean copulas.

Examples of bivariate Archimedean copulas

We now give examples of some families of Archimedean copulas which are commonly encountered; the Gumbel, the Clayton and the Frank families. As we will see in section 4.8 on page 61, they provide us with a set of very different dependence structures. The Clayton copula has lower tail dependence for $\alpha > 0$ and can be useful in situations where extreme negative events appear to occur together, as in dependent defaults; the Gumbel copula has upper tail dependence and is therefore a candidate where extreme positive events appear to occur simultaneously, as in a portfolio of dependent insurance losses; the Frank copula is symmetric and provides no tail dependence.

Example 4.4.5: Gumbel family

The generator function for the Gumbel family is

$$\varphi_\alpha(t) = (-\ln t)^\alpha, \quad \text{for } \alpha \geq 1. \tag{4.28}$$

We see that $\varphi_\alpha(t)$ is continuous and $\varphi_\alpha(1) = 0$. The derivative with respect to t is

$$\varphi_\alpha'(t) = -\alpha(-\ln t)^{\alpha-1}\frac{1}{t}, \tag{4.29}$$

so φ is a strictly decreasing function from $[0,1]$ to $[0,\infty]$. Since $\varphi_\alpha''(t) \geq 0$ on $[0,1]$, we see that φ is convex. Moreover, since $\varphi_\alpha(0) = \infty$ we have that φ is a strict generator. Consequently, $\varphi^{[-1]} = \varphi^{-1}$.

From theorem 4.4.3 on the preceding page we get that

$$C_\alpha^{\text{GU}}(u_1, u_2) = \exp\left\{ -\left[(-\ln u_1)^\alpha + (-\ln u_2)^\alpha\right]^{\frac{1}{\alpha}} \right\}, \quad \text{for } \alpha \geq 1 \tag{4.30}$$

is a family of copulas, and this copula family is called the Gumbel family.

In the case where $\alpha = 1$ we obtain $\varphi_1(t) = -\ln(t)$, which is the generator of the independence copula; perfect positive dependence is obtained when $\alpha \to \infty$.

In figure 4.3a on the following page we see a scatterplot of simulated values from the bivariate Gumbel copula with $\alpha = 2$, and in figure 4.3b on the next page we have transformed the data using the quantile function of the standard normal distribution. We clearly see how the dependence increase in the upper tail.

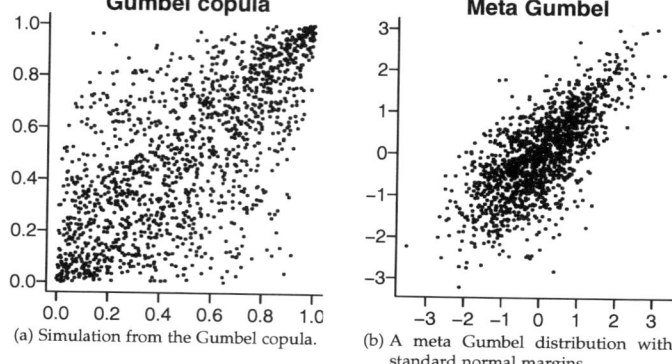

(a) Simulation from the Gumbel copula.

(b) A meta Gumbel distribution with standard normal margins.

Figure 4.3: Figure (a) shows a scatterplot of 1,500 simulated points from the bivariate Gumbel copula with $\alpha = 2$. In figure (b) we have transformed the data with the quantile function of the standard normal distribution. In both plots we clearly see the effect of the upper tail dependence.

Example 4.4.6: Frank family

The Frank family has generator function

$$\varphi_\alpha(t) = \ln \frac{e^{\alpha t} - 1}{e^\alpha - 1}, \quad \text{for } \alpha \in \mathbb{R}. \tag{4.31}$$

Again the generator function φ is continuous and $\varphi_\alpha(1) = 0$.
The derivative with respect to t is

$$\varphi_\alpha'(t) = -\frac{1}{\alpha} \ln[1 - (1 - e^{-\alpha})e^{-t}], \tag{4.32}$$

so φ is a strictly decreasing function from $[0,1]$ to $[0,\infty]$.

Since $\varphi_\alpha''(t) \geq 0$ on $[0,1]$ we see that φ is convex. Moreover, since $\varphi_\alpha(0) = \infty$, we have that φ is a strict generator. Consequently, the pseudo-inverse and the usual inverse are identical.

From theorem 4.4.3 on page 46 we get that

$$C_\alpha^{FR}(u_1, u_2) = -\frac{1}{\alpha} \ln \left(1 + \frac{(e^{-\alpha u_1} - 1)(e^{-\alpha u_2} - 1)}{e^{-\alpha} - 1} \right) \quad \text{for } \alpha \in \mathbb{R}, \quad (4.33)$$

is a family of copulas and this copula family is called the Frank family.

In the case where $\alpha = 0$, the generator function is taken to be the limit $\lim_{\alpha \to 0} \varphi_\alpha(t) = -\ln t$, which is the generator of the independence copula. Perfect negative and positive dependence are obtained for $\alpha \to -\infty$ and $\alpha \to \infty$, respectively.

The Frank copula is the only Archimedean copula with radial symmetry (definition A.2.3) such that $C_\alpha^{FR}(1 - u_1, 1 - u_2) = C_\alpha^{FR}(u_1, u_2)$, or, equivalently, that the survival copula (section 4.5) is equal to the copula of U. The properties of the Frank family is studied in Genest (1987), and the reader can refer to this article and the references therein for further details.

In figure 4.4a we see a scatterplot of simulated values from the bivariate Frank copula with $\alpha = 10$, and in figure 4.4b we have transformed the data using the quantile function of the standard normal distribution.

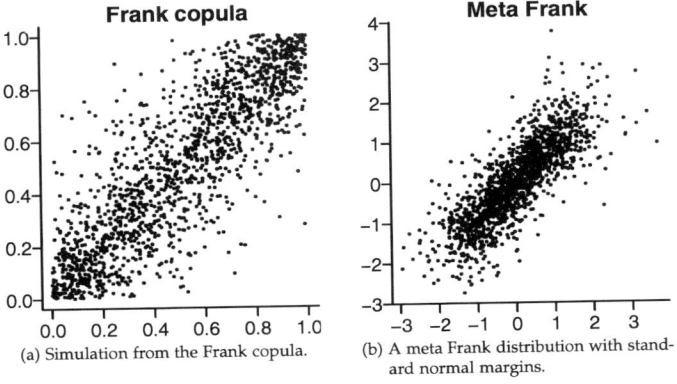

(a) Simulation from the Frank copula.

(b) A meta Frank distribution with standard normal margins.

Figure 4.4: Figure (a): a scatterplot of 1,500 simulated points from the bivariate Frank copula with $\alpha = 10$. In figure (b) we have transformed the data with the quantile function of the standard normal distribution.

Example 4.4.7: Clayton

The Clayton copula has generator function

$$\varphi_\alpha(t) = \frac{1}{\alpha}(t^{-\alpha} - 1), \quad \text{for } \alpha \geq -1. \tag{4.34}$$

Since $\varphi_\alpha(0) < \infty$ when $\alpha < 0$, this generator is only strict for $\alpha \geq 0$. As an illustration, consider $\alpha = -\frac{1}{2}$. Then we have $\varphi_{-\frac{1}{2}}(t)$ as a function from $[0,1]$ to $[0,2]$, and if we try to evaluate equation 4.26 on page 46 in a point where $\varphi(u_1) + \varphi(u_2) > 2$, the usual inverse $\varphi^{-1}(\varphi(u_1) + \varphi(u_2))$ is undefined. This is a situation where we need the definition of the pseudo-inverse (definition 4.4.1 on page 45). We get

$$C_\alpha^{\mathrm{CL}}(u_1, u_2) = \varphi^{[-1]}(\varphi(u_1) + \varphi(u_2)) \tag{4.35}$$

$$= \begin{cases} \varphi^{-1}(\varphi(u_1) + \varphi(u_2)), & \text{for } \varphi(u_1) + \varphi(u_2) \leq \varphi(0); \\ 0, & \text{otherwise.} \end{cases}$$

$$\tag{4.36}$$

$$= \max\left([u_1^{-\alpha} + u_2^{-\alpha} - 1]^{-\frac{1}{\alpha}}, 0\right), \quad \text{for } \alpha \geq -1. \tag{4.37}$$

When $\alpha = 0$, the generator function is again taken to be $\lim_{\alpha \to 0} \varphi_\alpha(t) = -\ln t$.

When $\alpha \geq 0$, the generator is strict and the expression for the copula simplifies to

$$C_\alpha^{\mathrm{CL}}(u_1, u_2) = (u_1^{-\alpha} + u_2^{-\alpha} - 1)^{-\frac{1}{\alpha}}. \tag{4.38}$$

This system were originally introduced by Clayton (1978).

In figure 4.5a on the next page we see a scatterplot of simulated values from the bivariate Clayton copula with $\alpha = 2$, and in figure 4.5b on the facing page we have transformed the data using the quantile function of the standard normal distribution. We clearly see how the dependence increase in the lower tail.

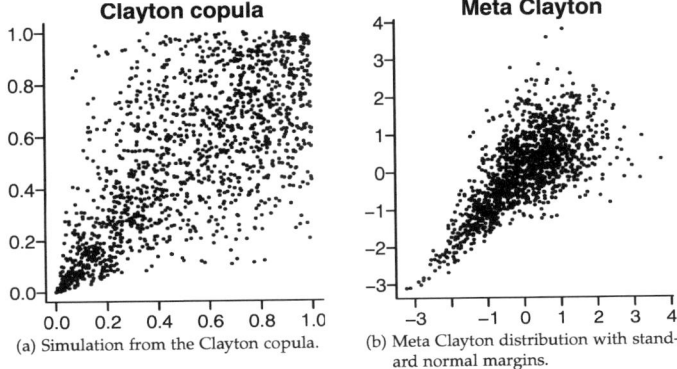

(a) Simulation from the Clayton copula.

(b) Meta Clayton distribution with standard normal margins.

Figure 4.5: Figure (a) shows a scatterplot of 1,500 simulated points from the bivariate Clayton copula with $\alpha = 2$. In figure (b) we have transformed the data with the quantile function of the standard normal distribution. In both plots we clearly see the effect of the lower tail dependence.

In table 4.1 we give a summary of the four Archimedean copulas we have studied so far, and in figure 4.6 on the following page we compare the scatterplots of the Gaussian, the Gumbel, the Clayton and the t-copula. All of them have approximately equal correlation of 0.7 and identical marginals, but it is quite clear that they have very different dependence structures.

Summary of bivariate Archimedean copulas

Family	Generator	Param.	Bivariate copula
Independent	$-\ln t$		$u_1 u_2$
Clayton	$\frac{1}{\alpha}(t^{-\alpha} - 1)$	$\alpha \geq -1$	$\max([u_1^{-\alpha} + u_2^{-\alpha} - 1]^{-\frac{1}{\alpha}}, 0)$
Gumbel	$(-\ln t)^\alpha$	$\alpha \geq 1$	$\exp\left\{-[(-\ln u_1)^\alpha + (-\ln u_2)^\alpha]^{\frac{1}{\alpha}}\right\}$
Frank	$\ln \frac{e^{\alpha t}-1}{e^\alpha-1}$	$\alpha \in \mathbb{R}$	$-\frac{1}{\alpha} \ln\left(1 + \frac{(e^{-\alpha u_1}-1)(e^{-\alpha u_2}-1)}{e^{-\alpha}-1}\right)$

Table 4.1: Summary of common bivariate Archimedean copulas. For details, see examples 4.4.5, 4.4.6 and 4.4.7.

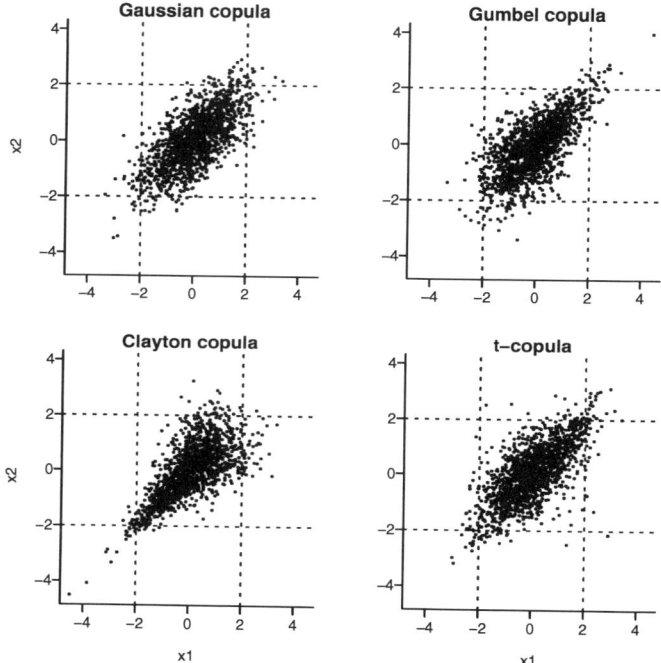

Figure 4.6: A comparison of the Gaussian, the Gumbel, the Clayton and the t-copula with standard normal margins. All of them are made such that they have a correlation of 0.7. Even though they have equal correlation and identical marginal distributions, they have a very different dependence structures. This plot is based on an example given in McNeil *et al.* (2005, pages 194–195).

Archimedean copulas for $d > 2$

For the generalization to more than two variables, we need some additional requirements on the generator function φ to make sure that

$$C(u_1, \ldots, u_d) = \varphi^{[-1]}\big(\varphi(u_1) + \cdots + \varphi(u_d)\big) \qquad (4.39)$$

defines a distribution function. It was shown by Kimberling (1974) that the generator function must be strict (definition 4.4.4) and completely monotonic (see below) on $\mathbb{I} = [0, 1]$. Note that since the generator has to be strict, $\varphi^{[-1]}$ will always be equal to φ^{-1} for Archimedean copulas with $d > 2$.

Definition 4.4.8: Completely monotonic

The function $\varphi(u)$ is completely monotonic on an interval, say $\mathbb{I} = [0, 1]$, if it is continuous there and has derivatives of all orders that alternate in sign. That is

$$(-1)^d \frac{\mathrm{d}^d}{\mathrm{d}u^d} \varphi^{-1}(u) \geq 0 \quad \text{for } d = 0, 1, 2, \ldots \qquad (4.40)$$

for all u in $[0, 1]$.

With this definition we can define multivariate Archimedean copulas for $d > 2$. A similar definition can be found in Nelsen (2006, page 152).

Definition 4.4.9: Archimedean copula

Let φ be a continuous strictly decreasing function from $\mathbb{I} = [0, 1]$ to $[0, \infty]$ such that $\varphi(0) = \infty$, $\varphi(1) = 0$. Let φ^{-1} be completely monotonic on $[0, \infty)$. Then the function defined by

$$C(u_1, \ldots, u_d) = \varphi^{-1}(\varphi(u_1) + \cdots + \varphi(u_d)), \qquad (4.41)$$

is an Archimedean copula for all $d \geq 2$.

Examples of multivariate Archimedean copulas for $d > 2$

Below we give four examples of common multivariate Archimedean copulas for $d > 2$. As will be seen, they are just generalizations of the bivariate copulas given above.

Example 4.4.10: Gumbel d-copula

In the case of the Gumbel copula, the generator function is given by $\varphi_\alpha(t) = (-\ln t)^\alpha$ for $\alpha \geq 1$. The generator $\varphi_\alpha(0) = \infty$ for all $\alpha \geq 0$, so the generator is strict. Since $\varphi_\alpha^{-1}(t)$ is completely monotonic on $[0, \infty)$ the Gumbel d-copula is given by the expression

$$C^{\text{GU}}(u_1, \ldots, u_d) = \exp\left\{ -\left[\sum_{i=1}^d (-\ln u_i)^\alpha \right]^{\frac{1}{\alpha}} \right\}, \quad \text{for } \alpha \geq 1. \tag{4.42}$$

In figure 4.7 we see a scatterplot of 1,500 simulated points from the 3-dimensional Gumbel copula with $\alpha = 2$ and standard normal margins.

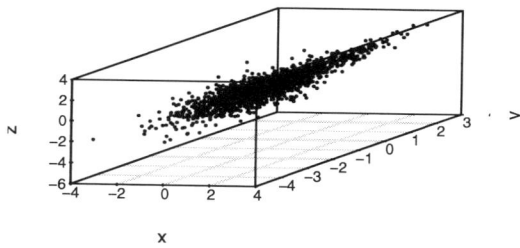

Figure 4.7: A scatterplot of 1,500 simulated points from the 3-dimensional Gumbel copula with $\alpha = 2$ and standard normal margins.

Example 4.4.11: Frank d-copula

In the case of the Frank copula, the generator function is given by $\varphi = \ln \frac{e^{\alpha t} - 1}{e^\alpha - 1}$ for $\alpha \in \mathbb{R}$. This generator is strict for all values of α, but

$$\varphi_\alpha^{-1}(t) = -\frac{1}{\alpha} \ln\left[1 - (1 - e^{-\alpha}) e^t \right] \tag{4.43}$$

fails to be completely monotonic when $\alpha < 0$ and the Frank d-copula is therefore only defined for $\alpha > 0$. The Frank d-copula is given by

$$C^{\text{FR}}(u_1, \ldots, u_d) = -\frac{1}{\alpha} \ln\left(1 + \frac{\prod_{i=1}^d (e^{\alpha u_i} - 1)}{(e^\alpha - 1)^{d-1}} \right), \quad \text{for } \alpha > 0. \tag{4.44}$$

54

In figure 4.8 we see a scatterplot of 1,500 simulated points from the 3-dimensional Frank copula with $\alpha = 10$ and standard normal margins.

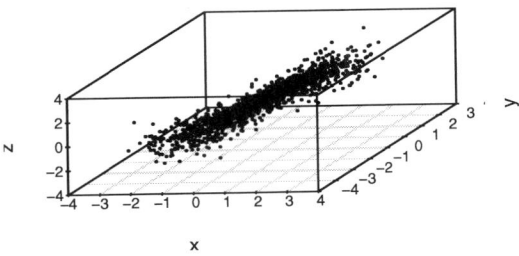

Figure 4.8: A scatterplot of 1,500 simulated points from the 3-dimensional Frank copula with $\alpha = 10$ and standard normal margins.

Example 4.4.12: Clayton d-copula

Let $\varphi_\alpha(t) = t^{-\alpha} - 1$ for $\alpha > 0$. The generator $\varphi_\alpha(0) = \infty$ for all $\alpha > 0$, so the generator is strict. Here $\varphi_\alpha^{-1}(t) = (1+t)^{-\frac{1}{\alpha}}$, which is completely monotonic on $[0, \infty)$. The Clayton d-copula is given by the expression

$$C^{\text{CL}}(u_1, \ldots, u_d) = \left(\sum_{i=1}^{d} u_i^{-\alpha} - d + 1 \right)^{-\frac{1}{\alpha}} \quad \text{for } \alpha > 0. \quad (4.45)$$

In figure 4.9 we see a scatterplot of 1,500 simulated points from the 3-dimensional Clayton copula with $\alpha = 2.2$ and standard normal margins.

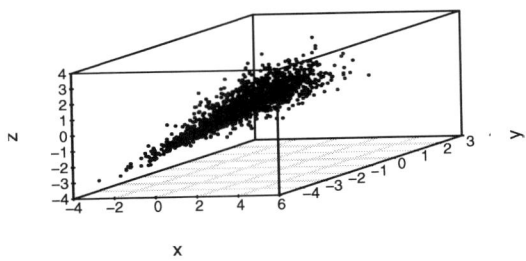

Figure 4.9: A scatterplot of 1,500 simulated points from the 3-dimensional Clayton copula with $\alpha = 2.2$. and standard normal margins.

4.5 Survival copulas

The survival copula is useful since it can be used to introduce *dependence* between survival times. This is of particular interest in survival modelling and in credit risk models.

Let X be a random vector with multivariate survival function

$$\bar{F} = \mathbb{P}(X_1 > x_1, \ldots, X_d > x_d) \tag{4.46}$$

and marginal survival functions $\bar{F}_1, \ldots, \bar{F}_d$, where $\bar{F}_i = 1 - F_i$. The survival copula is then the function which couples the *univariate* survival functions to their *multivariate* survival functions. When $F_1, \ldots, F_d$ are continuous, we can easily find the survival copula.

$$\bar{F}(x_1 \ldots, x_d) = \mathbb{P}(X_1 > x_1, \ldots, X_d > x_d) \tag{4.47}$$
$$= \mathbb{P}(\bar{F}_1(X_1) \leq \bar{F}_1(x_1), \ldots, \bar{F}_d(X_d) \leq \bar{F}_d(x_d)) \tag{4.48}$$
$$= \widehat{C}(\bar{F}_1(x_1), \ldots, \bar{F}_d(x_d)) \tag{4.49}$$

The survival copula is denoted $\widehat{C}$ and should not be confused with the survival function, $\overline{C} = \mathbb{P}(U_1 > u_1, \ldots, U_d > u_d)$, of d uniform $(0,1)$ random variables. We state a relation between the survival copula and the survival function. See McNeil *et al.* (2005, page 196).

$$\overline{C}(u_1, \ldots, u_d) = \mathbb{P}(U_1 > u_1, \ldots, U_d > u_d) \tag{4.50}$$
$$= \mathbb{P}(1 - U_1 \leq 1 - u_1, \ldots, 1 - U_d \leq 1 - u_d) \tag{4.51}$$
$$= \widehat{C}(1 - u_1, \ldots, 1 - u_d). \tag{4.52}$$

Note that when the distribution of X is elliptical, or more generally, when the random vector is radially symmetric (definition A.2.3 on page 102), the copula C of X is identical to the survival copula $\widehat{C}$ of X. In situations like this we can equally well work with the copula as the survival copula.

4.6 Extreme value copulas

This section relies on the extreme value theory given in section 2.4 on page 16, and the reader may refer to this part of the thesis if necessary.

In the section of multivariate extreme value (MEV) theory (section 2.4.2 on page 19) we saw that if G is a MEV distribution, then it must have univariate margins belonging to the generalized extreme value distributions defined in theorem 2.4.1 on page 16. Since these are continuous, Sklar's theorem guarantees that G has a unique copula.

If the limit in equation 2.19 on page 20 exists, then

$$G(x) = C(G_{\gamma_1}(x_1), \ldots, G_{\gamma_d}(x_d)),\qquad(4.53)$$

where $G_{\gamma_i}(x_i)$, $i = 1, \ldots, d$ are the univariate extreme value distributions defined in equation 2.14 on page 17.

Theorem 4.6.1: Extreme value copula

Suppose that F is in the domain of attraction of an multivariate extreme value distribution, written $F \in \mathrm{MDA}(G)$, such that

$$G(x) = C(G_{\gamma_1}(x_1), \ldots, G_{\gamma_d}(x_d)).\qquad(4.54)$$

Then the copula C of F satisfies

$$C(u^t) = C(u)^t, \quad \text{for all } t > 0.\qquad(4.55)$$

Every copula satisfying equation 4.55 is called an extreme value copula and can be a copula of an extreme value distribution (McNeil *et al.* 2005, page 312).

We also have that every distribution function G having an extreme value copula and margins belonging to the generalized extreme value distributions is an extreme value distribution.

Below we give two examples of extreme value copulas. This is not a complete list of extreme value copulas, but a list of the ones presented in this thesis.

Example 4.6.2: The independence copula

The independence copula (equation 4.61 on the next page) obviously satisfies equation 4.55. We have that

$$\Pi^t(u) = \left(\prod_{i=1}^{d} u_i\right)^t = \Pi(u^t).\qquad(4.56)$$

Example 4.6.3: Gumbel copula

The Gumbel copula is also an extreme value copula. we have that

$$C_\alpha^{GU}(\boldsymbol{u})^t = \exp\left\{-t\left[(-\ln u_1)^\alpha + \cdots + (-\ln u_d)^\alpha\right]^{\frac{1}{\alpha}}\right\} \qquad (4.57)$$

$$= \exp\left\{-\left[(-t\ln u_1)^\alpha + \cdots + (-t\ln u_d)^\alpha\right]^{\frac{1}{\alpha}}\right\} \qquad (4.58)$$

$$= C_\alpha^{GU}(u_1^t, \ldots, u_d^t). \qquad (4.59)$$

4.7 Fundamental copulas and the Fréchet bounds

Let us look at some copulas that provide special cases of dependence: independence, perfect positive dependence and perfect negative dependence. These copulas are often referred to as fundamental copulas.

The continuous random variables $X_1, \ldots, X_d$ are independent if and only if

$$F(x_1, \ldots, x_d) = \prod_{i=1}^{d} F_i(x_i). \qquad (4.60)$$

We see that the random variables are independent if and only if their copula is the independence copula

$$\Pi(u_1, \ldots, u_d) = \prod_{i=1}^{d} u_i, \qquad (4.61)$$

where Π is a common notation for this particular copula. Note that we have already presented the independence copula in equations 4.22 and 4.23.

It is also straightforward to show that the joint distribution function is bounded by the so called Fréchet bounds. In fact, if we consider the random variables $X_1, \ldots, X_d$ with continuous distribution functions $F_1, \ldots, F_d$, then

$$F(x_1, \ldots, x_d) \leq \min(F_1(x_1), \ldots, F_d(x_d)), \qquad (4.62)$$

which gives an upper bound on the joint distribution function.

A lower bound is derived with the following calculations.

$$F_X(x) = 1 - \bar{F}_X(x) \tag{4.63}$$

$$\geq 1 - (\bar{F}_1(x_1) + \cdots + \bar{F}_d(x_d)) \tag{4.64}$$

$$\geq 1 - (1 - F_1(x_1) + \cdots + 1 - F_d(x_d)) \tag{4.65}$$

$$= F_1(x_1) + \cdots + F_d(x_d) + 1 - d, \tag{4.66}$$

and this gives

$$F(x_1, \ldots, x_d) \geq \max(F_1(x_1) + \cdots + F_d(x_d) + 1 - d, 0). \tag{4.67}$$

Clearly, the lower and upper bound for the joint distribution function hold for copulas as well. We get that

$$\max(u_1 + \cdots + u_d + 1 - d, 0) \leq C(u_1, \ldots, u_d) \leq \min(u_1, \ldots, u_d), \tag{4.68}$$

and these bounds are often written as

$$W(u_1, \ldots, u_d) \leq C(u_1, \ldots, u_d) \leq M(u_1, \ldots, u_d). \tag{4.69}$$

The upper bound, $M(u_1, \ldots, u_d)$, always satisfies the definition of a copula.

The lower bound, $W(u_1, \ldots, u_d)$, only satisfies the definition of a copula when $d = 2$. Nevertheless, it is still the best possible lower bound, in the meaning that for each u, there exists a copula C with $C(u) = W(u)$ (Nelsen 2006, page 48).

Theorem 4.7.1: Perfect positive dependence (comonotonicity copula)

For $d \geq 2$, let $X = (X_1, \ldots, X_d)'$ be continuous random variables. Then the copula of X is the Fréchet upper bound M if and only if the random variables are almost surely a strictly increasing function of any of the others. In other words, the comonotonicity copula is the Fréchet upper bound copula from equation 4.69.

Theorem 4.7.2: Perfect negative dependence (countermonotonicity copula)

The Fréchet lower bound is not a valid copula for $d > 2$, and the counter-monotonicity copula is only defined for $d = 2$. Let X_1 and X_2 be continuous random variables. Then the copula of $X = (X_1, X_2)'$ is the Fréchet lower bound W if and only if X_1 is almost surely a strictly decreasing function of X_2. In other words, the countermonotonicity copula is the two dimensional Fréchet lower bound $W(u_1, u_2) = \max(u_1 + u_2 - 1, 0)$ from equation 4.69 on the preceding page.

Special cases

In the Gaussian copula the dependence is given in the correlation matrix $\boldsymbol{R}$. If the correlation matrix is the identity matrix $\boldsymbol{R} = I_d$, we obtain the independence copula Π; if $\boldsymbol{R}$ consists entirely of ones, we obtain the upper Fréchet bound M, in other words, perfect positive dependence. For $d = 2$ we also have that the Gaussian copula is equal to the lower Fréchet bound W when $\rho = -1$, that is, perfect negative dependence. We say that the dependence in the Gaussian copula interpolates between perfect negative and perfect positive dependence.

As for the Gaussian copula, the t-copula gives perfect positive dependence when $\boldsymbol{R}$ consists entirely of ones; however, if $\boldsymbol{R} = I_d$, we do not obtain the independence copula (for $v < \infty$). This is because uncorrelated multivariate t-distributed random variables are not independent (see section 2.3.1 on page 13).

In table 4.2 we show that independence, comonotonicity and countermonotonicity are special cases of the bivariate Archimedean copulas (given in section 4.4 on page 45). We see from this table how the dependence interpolates between perfect negative dependence, independence and perfect positive dependence with the choice of the parameter α.

Limiting and special cases		
Family	Param	Limiting and special cases
Clayton	$\alpha \geq -1$	$C_{-1} = W, \quad C_0 = \Pi, \quad C_\infty = M$
Frank	$\alpha \in \mathbb{R}$	$C_{-\infty} = W, \quad C_0 = \Pi, \quad C_\infty = M$
Gumbel	$\alpha \geq 1$	$C_1 = \Pi, \quad C_\infty = M$

Table 4.2: Limiting and special cases of bivariate Archimedean copulas. We see how the dependence interpolates between perfect negative dependence, independence and perfect positive dependence.

4.8 Dependence measures and copulas

In this section we will show how dependence measures like the correlation coefficient, rank correlations and the tail dependence are related to the parameters of the copulas. In addition to this we introduce a more robust estimator of the correlation coefficient which can be useful if the data come from an elliptical, but nonnormal distribution.

Let X_1 and X_2 be random variables with continuous marginal distributions F_1 and F_2 and joint distribution F. It is interesting to examine whether traditional dependence concepts such as the Pearson's correlation, Kendall's τ and Spearman's ρ can be expressed in terms of the copula for F.

From lemmas 3.1.3, 3.1.6 and 3.1.8 we have that the Pearson's correlation is given by

$$\rho(X_1, X_2) = \frac{1}{\mathrm{SD}(X_1)\,\mathrm{SD}(X_2)} \int_{-\infty}^{\infty} \int_{-\infty}^{\infty} [F(x_1, x_2) - F_1(x_1)F_2(x_2)]\,dx_1\,dx_2,$$
(4.70)

Kendall's τ is given by

$$\tau(X_1, X_2) = 4 \int_{-\infty}^{\infty} \int_{-\infty}^{\infty} F(x_1, x_2)\,dF(x_1, x_2) - 1,$$
(4.71)

and Spearman's ρ by

$$\rho_s(X_1, X_2) = 12 \int_{-\infty}^{\infty} \int_{-\infty}^{\infty} [F(x_1, x_2) - F_1(x_1)F_2(x_2)]\,dF_1(x_1)\,dF_2(x_2).$$
(4.72)

Applying the probability integral transformation (theorem 2.1.2 on page 5) and letting $u_1 = F_1(x_1)$ and $u_2 = F_2(x_2)$, we obtain

$$\rho(X_1, X_2) = \frac{\int_0^1 \int_0^1 [C(u_1, u_2) - u_1 u_2]\,dF_1^{\leftarrow}(u_1)\,dF_2^{\leftarrow}(u_2)}{\mathrm{SD}(X_1)\,\mathrm{SD}(X_2)},$$
(4.73)

$$\tau(X_1, X_2) = 4 \int_0^1 \int_0^1 C(u_1, u_2)\,dC(u_1, u_2) - 1,$$
(4.74)

$$\rho_s(X_1, X_2) = 12 \int_0^1 \int_0^1 [C(u_1, u_2) - u_1 u_2]\,du_1\,du_2.$$
(4.75)

We see that Kendall's τ and Spearman's ρ are functions of the copula of X_1 and X_2 alone, while the Pearson linear correlation coefficient depends on the marginals as well.

Since rank correlations can be expressed as functions of the copula alone, it is interesting to see if we can express the parameters in the copula as a function of rank correlations. Below we show this connection for the most common copulas. The results will be used in section 5.1 on page 74 were we will see how these relationship can be used to calibrate the parameters of the copula.

First, we present the relationship for the implicit copulas, then, we present the relationship for the Archimedean copulas.

4.8.1 Rank correlation and copulas

In the case of the Gaussian copula there exists a relationship between the rank correlations and the linear correlation. We state this relationship as a theorem.

Theorem 4.8.1: Rank correlations for the Gaussian copula

Let (X_1, X_2) have a bivariate Gaussian copula and arbitrary continuous margins. Then the rank correlations are

$$\tau(X_1, X_2) = \frac{2}{\pi} \arcsin \rho, \tag{4.76}$$

and

$$\rho_s(X_1, X_2) = \frac{6}{\pi} \arcsin \frac{\rho}{2}, \tag{4.77}$$

where ρ is the correlation between X_1 and X_2.

Proof: See McNeil *et al.* (2005, pages 215–216).

The relationship between Kendall's τ and the correlation, given in equation 4.76, holds more generally for the copulas of all elliptical distributions (section 2.2), such as the *t*-copula (Lindskog *et al.* 2003). This can be used to build a robust estimator of linear correlation. By simply substituting the empirical value of τ into equation 4.76 and solving for ρ, we get

$$\widehat{\rho} = \sin(\frac{1}{2}\pi\widehat{\tau}). \tag{4.78}$$

Simulation studies shows that this simple estimator performs better than most of its competitors for data with nonnormal but elliptical distributions. See Lindskog *et al.* (2003) for further details.

In figure 4.10 on the following page we have compared the standard estimator of correlation with this robust estimator. The plots show 3,000 estimates from independent samples of size 100 from a bivariate t_4 distribution with correlation 0.5. We see from the plots that the robust estimator based on Kendall's τ outperforms the usual estimator in this situation. The mean from both estimators is approximately 0.5 but the variance is higher in the usual estimator, 0.017 against 0.008. In example 5.1.3 on page 77 we will use the robust estimator to estimate the correlation in copulas where the data are non-normal.

It is also possible to express the parameter in Archimedean copulas as a function of the rank correlations. These expressions involve the computation of a double integral; however, Genest and MacKay (1986) showed that there exists a simple expression for Kendall's τ when the copula belongs to the Archimedean family. We state this as a theorem.

Theorem 4.8.2

Let (X_1, X_2) be a random vector whose joint distribution is of the form of equation 4.26 on page 46 with an generator function φ. Then

$$\tau(X_1, X_2) = 4 \int_0^1 \frac{\varphi(t)}{\varphi'(t)} \, dt + 1. \tag{4.79}$$

Proof: See Genest and MacKay (1986) or Nelsen (2006, page 163).

With these two expressions it is possible to show that there exists a one-to-one relationsship between the parameters α and τ. We have summarized this relationship for some of the Archimedean copulas in table 4.3. See Frees and Valdez (1998) for further details.

The Archimedean copulas and Kendall's τ

Family	Parameter	Kendall's τ
Clayton	$\alpha > -1$	$\frac{\alpha}{\alpha+2}$
Gumbel	$\alpha > 1$	$\frac{\alpha-1}{\alpha}$
Frank	$\alpha \in \mathbb{R}$	$1 - \frac{4}{\alpha}\left(1 - D_1(\alpha)\right)$

Table 4.3: The relation between the dependence parameter α and Kendall's τ in some of the most common Archimedean copulas. D is the Debye function and $D_1(x) = \frac{1}{x}\int_0^x \frac{t}{e^t-1} \, dt$.

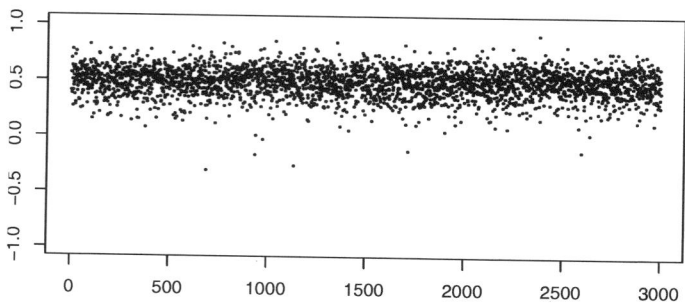

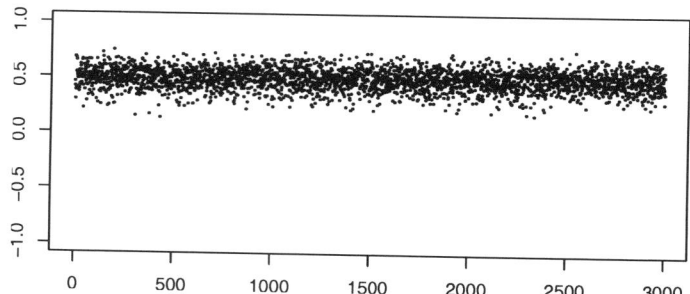

Figure 4.10: The usual estimator of correlation compared with the estimator based on Kendall's tau. The data consists of 3,000 samples of size 100 from a bivariate t_4 distribution with linear correlation 0.5. We see that the robust estimator outperforms the usual estimator in this simulation study. This is based on an example given in Lindskog *et al.* (2003).

4.8.2 Tail dependence and copulas

Let us again consider $X_1 \sim F_1$ and $X_2 \sim F_2$. If F_1 and F_2 are continuous, we can express the upper and lower tail dependence coefficients in terms of the copula of (X_1, X_2).

The lower tail dependence coefficient (equation 3.17) can be written as

$$\lambda_l = \lim_{q \to 0} \mathbb{P}(F_1(X_1) \leq q \mid F_2(X_2) \leq q) \tag{4.80}$$

$$= \lim_{q \to 0} \frac{\mathbb{P}(F_1(X_1) \leq q, F_2(X_2) \leq q)}{\mathbb{P}(F_2(X_2) \leq q)} \tag{4.81}$$

$$= \lim_{q \to 0} \frac{C(q, q)}{q}, \tag{4.82}$$

and similar for the upper tail dependence coefficient (equation 3.16)

$$\lambda_u = \lim_{q \to 1} \frac{\mathbb{P}(F_1(X_1) > q, F_2(X_2) > q)}{\mathbb{P}(F_2(X_2) > q)} \tag{4.83}$$

$$= \lim_{q \to 1} \frac{\overline{C}(q, q)}{1 - q} \tag{4.84}$$

$$= \lim_{q \to 1} \frac{\widehat{C}(1 - q, 1 - q)}{1 - q} \tag{4.85}$$

$$= \lim_{q \to 0} \frac{\widehat{C}(q, q)}{q}, \tag{4.86}$$

where $\overline{C}$ is the survival function of uniform random variables and $\widehat{C}$ is the survival copula of C (section 4.5). Equation 4.85 follows from the relation given in equation 4.52 on page 56.

The concept of lower tail dependence can be defined in an alternative way that is useful for copulas without a simple closed form expression. By applying L'Hôpital's rule and the definition of the conditional copula (section A.5) we get that (McNeil *et al.* (2005))

$$\lambda_l = \lim_{q \to 0} \frac{C(q, q)}{q} = \lim_{q \to 0} \frac{dC(q, q)}{dq} \tag{4.87}$$

$$= \lim_{q \to 0} \mathbb{P}(U_1 \leq q \mid U_2 = q) + \lim_{q \to 0} \mathbb{P}(U_2 \leq q \mid U_1 = q). \tag{4.88}$$

If C is exchangeable copula (definition A.3.1) such that $C(u_1, u_2) = C(u_2, u_1)$, then equation 4.88 on the preceding page simplifies to

$$\lambda_l = 2 \lim_{q \to 0} \mathbb{P}(U_1 \leq q \mid U_2 = q). \tag{4.89}$$

For radially symmetric copulas (definition A.2.3 on page 102), we have that $\widehat{C} = C$. For these copulas we get $\lambda_u = \lambda_l$.

We will now use equation 4.89 to calculate the tail dependence in the Gaussian and in the t-copula.

Tail dependence in implicit copulas

Both the Gaussian and the t-copula are symmetric (definition A.2.3); in fact, every copula derived from a normal variance mixture (definition 2.3.1) have radial symmetry, and in these situations we do not have to calculate both the upper and lower tail dependence.

Example 4.8.3: Tail dependence in the Gaussian copula

In this example we use equation 4.89 to show that the Gaussian copula have asymptotic independence: Extreme events appear to occur independently in each margin.

Let the random vector (X_1, X_2) have the Gaussian copula. Since the Gaussian copula is exchangeable (definition A.3.1) and symmetric, the coefficient of upper and lower tail dependence is given by

$$\lambda_l = 2 \lim_{q \to 0} \mathbb{P}(U_1 \leq q \mid U_2 = q) \tag{4.90}$$

$$= 2 \lim_{q \to 0} \mathbb{P}(\Phi^{-1}(U_1) \leq \Phi^{-1}(q) \mid \Phi^{-1}(U_2) = \Phi^{-1}(q)) \tag{4.91}$$

$$= 2 \lim_{x \to -\infty} \mathbb{P}(X_1 \leq x \mid X_1 = x) \tag{4.92}$$

Since $X_1 \mid X_2 = X \sim N(\rho X, 1 - \rho^2)$ we obtain

$$\lambda = 2 \lim_{x \to -\infty} \Phi\left(\frac{x - \rho x}{\sqrt{1 - \rho^2}}\right) = 2 \lim_{x \to -\infty} \Phi\left(x \frac{\sqrt{1 - \rho}}{\sqrt{1 + \rho}}\right) = 0, \tag{4.93}$$

provided that $\rho < 1$. In other words, the Gaussian copula is assymptotically independent in the tails.

Example 4.8.4: Tail dependence in the *t*-copula

Embrechts *et al.* (2002) showed, in a similar way as for the Gaussian copula, that the tail dependence in the *t*-copula is

$$\lambda = 2t_{\nu+1}\left(-\sqrt{\frac{(\nu+1)(1-\rho)}{1+\rho}}\right),\qquad(4.94)$$

where $t_{\nu+1}$ denotes the univariate *t*-distribution with $\nu+1$ degrees of freedom.

Provided that $\rho > -1$ we see that the *t*-copula is asymptotically dependent in the tails.

In figure 4.11 we see how the tail dependence increases as ν decreases and/or ρ increases. Note that even for zero or negative correlation there is some tail dependence. This is because all the variables are related to the same random variable W (see section 2.3.1 on page 13, for details).

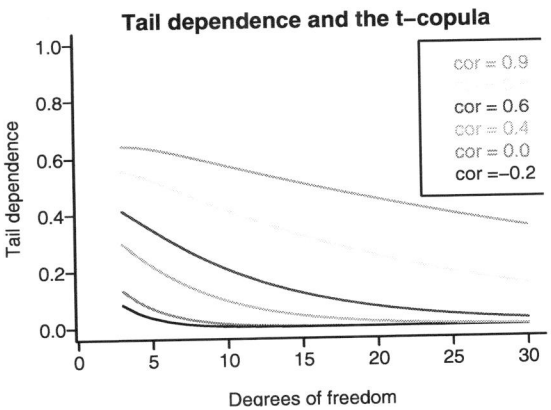

Figure 4.11: A plot of the tail dependence against the degrees of freedom at various levels of correlation in the *t*-distribution. Note that even for negative correlation values there is some tail dependence.

The tail dependence for the Clayton and the Gumbel copula can be calculated from equation 4.82 and equation 4.86, respectively. The results are presented in table 4.4. In figure 4.3 on page 48 we see the effect of the upper tail dependence in the Gumbel copula and in figure 4.5 on page 51 we see the effect of the lower tail dependence in the Clayton copula.

See McNeil *et al.* (2005, pages 208–210) for further details.

The Archimedean copulas and tail dependence

Family	Parameter	λ_u	λ_l
Clayton	$\alpha > -1$	0	$\begin{cases} 2^{-\frac{1}{\alpha}}, & \alpha > 0 \\ 0, & \alpha \leq 0 \end{cases}$
Gumbel	$\alpha > 1$	$2 - 2^{\frac{1}{\alpha}}$	0
Frank	$\alpha \in \mathbb{R}$	0	0

Table 4.4: The relation between the dependence parameter α and the tail dependence coefficient in some of the most common Archimedean copulas.

4.9 Dependence maps

To visually explore the effect the different copulas has on the dependence, we have produced dependence maps (see section 3.2.1 on page 28) on simulated values from meta distributions constructed by the Clayton, the Gaussian, the t and the Gumbel copula, respectively. The plots are found in figure 4.12 on the facing page to figure 4.15 on page 72. It is interesting to see that the dependence maps captures the increasing dependence in the tail for the Clayton, the t, and the Gumbel copula.

Again, all of the distributions have the same standard normal marginal distributions and approximately equal correlation coefficients, but, we see that they have very different dependence structures.

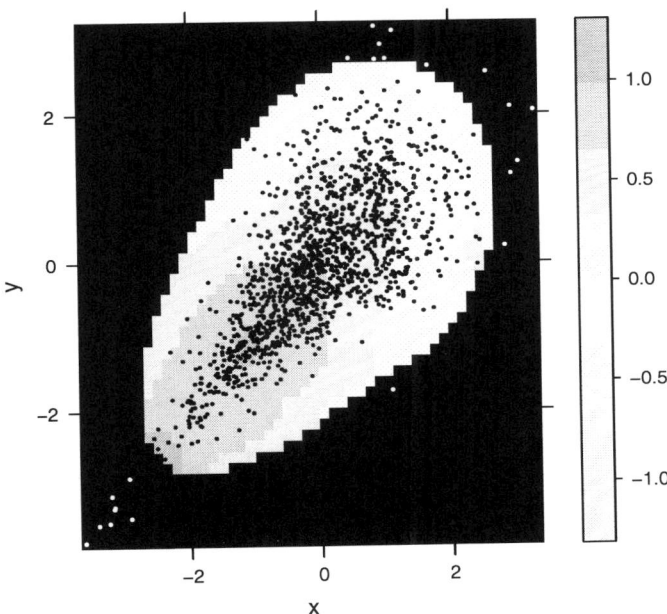

Figure 4.12: Dependence map: A plot of 1,500 simulated points from the bivariate Clayton copula with $\alpha = 2.2$ and standard normal margins. We see that there is a clear indication of an increasing dependence in the lower tail.

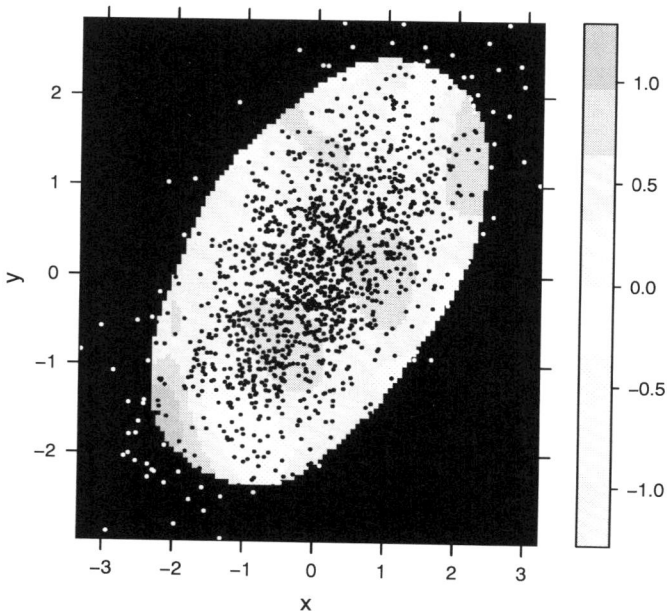

Figure 4.13: Dependence map: A plot of 1,500 simulated points from the bivariate Gaussian copula with $\rho = 0.7$ and standard normal margins. This is equivalent to the usual bivariate normal distribution. We see that this plot does not indicate a systematic trend of increasing dependence in the tails.

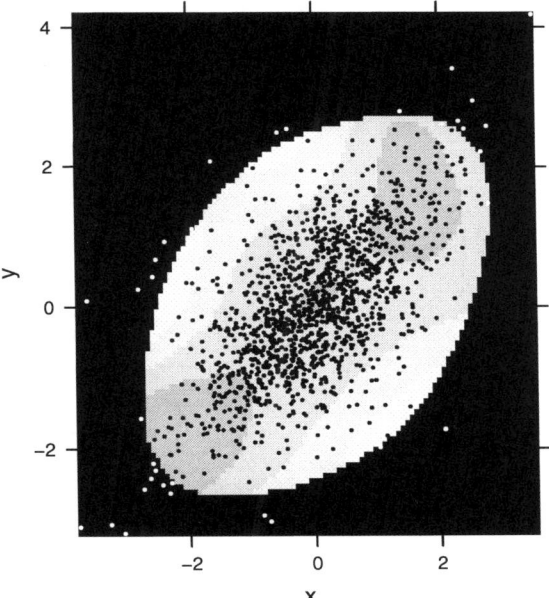

Figure 4.14: Dependence map: A plot of 1,500 simulated points from the bivariate t-copula with $\rho = 0.7$ and $\nu = 4$ and standard normal margins. We see that there is a clear indication of an increasing dependence in the upper and lower tails of the distribution.

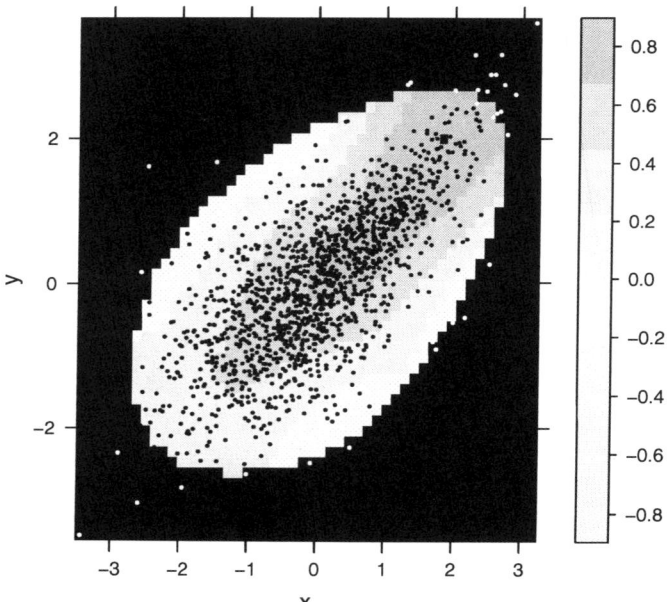

Figure 4.15: Dependence map: A plot of 1,500 simulated points from the bivariate Gumbel copula with $\alpha = 2$ and standard normal margins. We see that there is a clear indication of an increasing dependence in the upper tail.

5

Estimation procedures

In this chapter we will describe several methods that is used to estimate the parameters in a copula. To illustrate the problem we consider a copula C such that

$$F(x; \theta_1, \ldots, \theta_d, \alpha) = C(F_1(x_1; \theta_1), \ldots, F_d(x_d; \theta_d); \alpha), \quad (5.1)$$

where $\theta_1, \ldots, \theta_d$ are the parameters in the marginal distributions, and the copula C is parametrized by the parameter α.

We will present four methods of estimating some or all of the parameters: first we present the method of moments (section 5.1), and then we present three approaches based on maximum likelihood (section 5.2).

The maximum likelihood approaches are only different in the way they treat the marginal distributions. The first approach, given in section 5.2 on page 78, is to estimate the parameters in the copula and the parameters in the marginal distributions in one operation. Since we specify the parameters to be estimated a priori, this method is fully parametric.

In section 5.2.1 on page 79 we present another approach called inference functions for margins, or just IFM. This approach can be summarized in the following way: first we estimate the marginal distributions by some univariate statistical method, and then we estimate the parameters in the copula given the marginals by maximum likelihood. With this method we separate the estimation of the marginals and the dependence structure. Since we specify the parameters a priori, this is also a fully parametric method.

An alternative technique called the pseudo-likelihood, canonical maximum likelihood (CML) or just the semi-parametric approach is found in section 5.2.2 on page 80. It is a semi-parametric approach because we estimate the marginals non-parametrically and use the results in the estimation of the copula parameters. The advantage of this technique is that we do not run the risk of misspecifying the marginals; the disadvantage is that we can loose some information, especially in the tails of the marginal distributions.

In the above mentioned estimation procedures we have to choose a parametric model for either just the copula or the copula and the marginal distribution. These choices can be highly subjective, and it is of course important that we have a good reason to select the chosen model. We quote McNeil *et al.* (2005) on this:

> Obviously we assume that there are *a priori* grounds for considering the chosen copula to be an appropriate model, such as symmetry or the lack of it and the presence or absence of tail dependence.

In section 5.3 on page 85 we introduce a completely non-parametric method. The advantage of this is that we do not have to make any assumptions on the copula or the marginals. But, as in all non-parametric methods, we risk losing information from the tails of the distributions where the amount of data is often insufficient.

Let $X = (X_1, \ldots, X_d)'$ denote a generic random vector with multivariate distribution function F and continuous marginal distribution functions $F_1, \ldots, F_d$. Throughout this chapter we assume that we have n independent copies of X, denoted $X_1, \ldots, X_n$, where $X_j = (X_{j,1}, \ldots, X_{j,d})'$ for $j = 1, \ldots, n$ is an individual data vector. One interpretation can be that they represent daily losses over n days for d different risk factors. Since we assume that the marginals are continuous, Sklar's theorem (theorem 4.2.1 on page 39) guarantees that the copula of X is unique.

5.1 Moment estimators

In section 4.8 on page 61 we saw that there sometimes exists a theoretical relationship between the rank correlations and the parameters of the copula.

By simply substituting the empirical values of the rank correlations into this relationship, and solving for α we obtain an estimate of the copula parameter. This method was introduced by Genest and Rivest (1993), and is referred to as the method of moments.

5.1.1 Kendall's tau

Kendall's τ is especially important. From theorem 4.8.2 we see that we can write Kendall's τ as a function of the parameter of a bivariate Archimedean copula. These relationships are summarized in table 4.3 on page 63. We have also seen that equation 4.76 gives us a relationship between Kendall's τ and the correlation matrix R for copulas of all elliptical distributions (Lindskog et al. 2003).

We illustrate the method of moment with some examples.

Example 5.1.1: Clayton copula

Let (X_1, X_2) have the Clayton copula given in example 4.4.7 on page 50 such that

$$F(x_1, x_2) = C_\alpha^{\text{CL}}(F_1(x_1), F_2(x_2)), \quad \text{for } \alpha > -1. \tag{5.2}$$

Then we saw in table 4.3 on page 63 that Kendall's τ can be expressed as a function of the parameter α in the following way.

$$\tau(X_1, X_2) = \frac{\alpha}{\alpha + 2} \quad \text{for } \alpha > -1. \tag{5.3}$$

Substituting the estimate of Kendall's τ and solving for α gives us an estimated value of the parameter in the Clayton copula,

$$\widehat{\alpha} = \frac{2\widehat{\tau}}{1 - \widehat{\tau}}. \tag{5.4}$$

We saw in table 4.2 on page 60 that Clayton's copula interpolates between perfect negative and perfect positive dependence. If $\widehat{\tau} = -1$ then $\widehat{\alpha} = -1$, and we know that $C_{-1}^{\text{CL}} = W$; in other words, perfect negative dependence is obtained. If $\widehat{\tau} \to 1$ then $\widehat{\alpha} \to \infty$, and we know that $C_\infty^{\text{CL}} = M$; in other words, perfect positive dependence is obtained. Consequently, any sample value of Kendall's τ will provide a 'reasonable' estimate of α.

If we take a look at table 3.1 on page 27 we find the sample value of Kendall's τ for three indices: FTSE100 (FTSE), Swiss Market Index (SMI) and Standard & Poor 500 (SP). We have used the relationship given above to get a pairwise estimate of α in the Clayton copula. The results from this can be found in table 5.1.

	FTSE	SMI	SP
FTSE	∞	1.92	0.78
SMI	1.92	∞	0.60
SP	0.78	0.60	∞

Table 5.1: The parameter in the Clayton copula estimated from Kendall's τ.

Example 5.1.2: Gumbel copula

Let (X_1, X_2) have the Gumbel copula given in example 4.4.5 on page 47 such that

$$F(x_1, x_2) = C_\alpha^{GU}(F_1(x_1), F_2(x_2)), \quad \text{for } \alpha \geq 1. \tag{5.5}$$

Then we saw in table 4.3 on page 63 that Kendall's τ can be expressed as a function of the parameter α in the following way.

$$\tau(X_1, X_2) = \frac{\alpha - 1}{\alpha} \quad \text{for } \alpha \geq 1. \tag{5.6}$$

Substituting the estimate of Kendall's τ and solving for α gives us an estimated value of the parameter in the Gumbel copula,

$$\widehat{\alpha} = \frac{1}{1 - \widehat{\tau}}. \tag{5.7}$$

We saw in table 4.2 on page 60 that Gumbel's copula interpolates between independence and perfect positive dependence. Since the Gumbel copula only provides positive dependence, the estimator is not defined, or assumed to be 1, for negative values of $\widehat{\tau}$. If $\widehat{\tau} = 0$, then $\widehat{\alpha} = 1$, and we know that $C_1^{GU} = \Pi$; that is, independence is obtained. If $\widehat{\tau} \to 1$, then $\widehat{\alpha} \to \infty$, and we know that perfect positive dependence is obtained when $\alpha \to \infty$. Consequently, only sample values of Kendall's $\tau \in [0, 1)$ will provide a 'reasonable' estimate of α.

If we take a look at table 3.1 on page 27, we find the value of Kendall's τ for three indices: FTSE100, Swiss Market Index and Standard & Poor 500.

We have used the relationship given above to get a pairwise estimate of α. The results can be found in table 5.2.

	FTSE	SMI	SP
FTSE	∞	1.96	1.39
SMI	1.96	∞	1.3
SP	1.39	1.3	∞

Table 5.2: The parameter of the Gumbel copula estimated from Kendall's τ.

Example 5.1.3: Normal-variance copulas

Let (X_1, X_2) have a copula derived from an elliptical distribution such as the t-copula (equation 4.19). Then we have from equation 4.76 on page 62 that

$$\tau(X_1, X_2) = \frac{2}{\pi} \arcsin \rho(X_1, X_2). \tag{5.8}$$

Substituting the sample value of Kendall's τ and solving for ρ gives us a robust estimate of the correlation between X_1 and X_2.

$$\widehat{\rho}^\star = \sin(\frac{1}{2}\pi\widehat{\tau}). \tag{5.9}$$

A possible estimator of the correlation matrix R is therefore obtained by performing this operation for all pairs of random variables in the sample. The results from this procedure can be found in table 5.5 on page 85. See figure 4.10 on page 64 for an illustration of the robustness of this estimator.

5.1.2 Spearman's rho

The general procedure is identical to the one for Kendall's τ, but the relationship between Spearman's ρ and the parameters in the copula is often complicated or not on a closed form. Still, Spearman's ρ gives us an estimate of the correlation matrix R of X if the copula of X is the Gaussian copula C_R^{GA}. We have from theorem 4.8.1 on page 62 that

$$\rho_s(X_1, X_2) = \frac{6}{\pi} \arcsin \frac{\rho}{2}. \tag{5.10}$$

This can give a robust estimator to the correlation if the data come from a Gaussian copula, with nonnormal margins. However, I have not been able to find any articles describing the properties of this estimator, nor of the usual estimator of ρ, in the case of the Gaussian copula.

5.2 Maximum Likelihood

Maximum likelihood is the dominating method in copula estimation. Consider the random vector $X = (X_1, \ldots, X_d)'$ with a parametrized copula, as in equation 5.1 on page 73. Assume that C has density c (section A.4) and that F_i has density f_i for $i = 1, \ldots, d$. Then X has density

$$f(x; \theta_1, \ldots, \theta_d, \alpha) = c\big(F_1(x_1; \theta_1), \ldots, F_d(x_d; \theta_d); \alpha\big) \prod_{i=1}^{d} f_i(x_i; \theta_i). \qquad (5.11)$$

Equation 5.11 is often referred to as the canonical representation, and is the starting point of any estimation method based on maximum likelihood.

Consider $X_1, \ldots, X_n$ as n i.i.d. realizations of the random vector $X = (X_1, \ldots, X_d)'$ with multivariate distribution function F and continuous marginal distribution functions $F_1, \ldots, F_d$. Then we have that the log-likelihood must be

$$l(\theta, \alpha) = \sum_{j=1}^{n} \ln c\big(F_1(x_{j,1}; \theta_1), \ldots, F_d(x_{j,d}; \theta_d); \alpha\big) + \sum_{j=1}^{n} \sum_{i=1}^{d} \ln f_i(x_{j,i}; \theta_i). \qquad (5.12)$$

Then, given a set of marginals and a copula, we get the maximum likelihood estimator as the argument that maximizes the log-likelihood

$$(\widehat{\theta}, \widehat{\alpha})_{\text{MLE}} = \arg\max_{\theta, \alpha} l(\theta, \alpha), \qquad (5.13)$$

where $\theta = (\theta_1, \ldots, \theta_d)$. This means that a possible candidate of the ML-estimator of (θ, α) can be found as the solution of

$$\left(\frac{\partial l}{\partial \theta_1}, \ldots, \frac{\partial l}{\partial \theta_d}, \frac{\partial l}{\partial \alpha} \right) = 0'. \qquad (5.14)$$

5.2.1 Inference functions for margins

The inference functions for margins (IFM) is described in Joe (1997, pages 299–316), or, alternatively, in Joe and Xu (1996). We see that equation 5.12 on the preceding page can be split into to parts, that is, we can separate the estimation of the parameters of the copula and the parameters of the marginal distributions.

First, we estimate the parameters of the marginals by maximum likelihood.

$$\widehat{\theta} = \arg\max_{\theta} \sum_{j=1}^{n} \sum_{i=1}^{d} \ln f_i(x_{j,i}; \theta_i). \tag{5.15}$$

This can obviously be done separately for all the d marginal distributions. Let $l_i(\theta_i) = \sum_{j=1}^{n} \ln f_i(x_{ji}; \theta_i)$ denote the log-likelihood of the ith margin. Then

$$\widehat{\theta}_i = \arg\max_{\theta_i} l_i(\theta_i) \tag{5.16}$$

$$= \arg\max_{\theta_i} \sum_{j=1}^{n} \ln f_i(x_{j,i}; \theta_i), \quad \text{for } i = 1, \ldots, d. \tag{5.17}$$

The next step is to use the above estimated parameters in the estimation of the parameters of the copula

$$\widehat{\alpha} = \arg\max_{\alpha} \sum_{j=1}^{n} \ln c(F_1(x_{j,1}; \widehat{\theta}_1), \ldots, F_d(x_{j,d}; \widehat{\theta}_d); \alpha). \tag{5.18}$$

With this method a possible candidate of the ML estimator of (θ, α) is the solution of

$$\left(\frac{\partial l_1}{\partial \theta_1}, \ldots, \frac{\partial l_d}{\partial \theta_d}, \frac{\partial l}{\partial \alpha} \right) = 0'. \tag{5.19}$$

According to Joe (1997), the IFM-method is computationally simpler than estimating all parameters $(\theta_1, \ldots, \theta_d, \alpha)$ simultaneously. A numerical method with many parameters is much more time consuming than several numerical optimizations, each with fewer parameters.

Joe (1997, chapter 10) also compares the exact ML-method with the IFM-method, and finds that the latter is highly efficient compared with the former. They also shows that the IFM-estimator is asymptotically normal under some regularity conditions.

5.2.2 Semi parametric method

The semi-parametric method, also known as the pseudo-likelihood or canonical maximum likelihood, is described in Genest *et al.* (1995). We keep the parametric form of the copula, but instead of specifying the marginals, we transform the data into uniform variables by using the empirical distribution function. The empirical distribution function based on the sample $x_{1,i}, \ldots, x_{n,i}$ is given by

$$\widehat{F}_{n,i}(x) = \frac{\text{number of elements less than or equal to } x}{n+1} \tag{5.20}$$

$$= \frac{1}{n+1} \sum_{j=1}^{n} I\{X_{j,i} \leq x\}, \tag{5.21}$$

where $I\{X_{j,i} \leq x\}$ is an indicator function returning

$$I\{X_{j,i} \leq x\} = \begin{cases} 1, & \text{if } X_{j,i} \leq x; \\ 0, & \text{if } X_{j,i} > x. \end{cases} \tag{5.22}$$

We divide by $n+1$ to avoid problems since the copula density may be infinite at the boundaries of $\mathbb{I} = [0,1]$ (Genest *et al.* 1995).

The next step is to estimate the copula parameters by maximum likelihood

$$\widehat{\boldsymbol{\alpha}} = \arg\max_{\boldsymbol{\alpha}} \sum_{j=1}^{n} \ln c(\widehat{F}_{n,1}(x_{j,1}), \ldots, \widehat{F}_{n,d}(x_{j,d}); \boldsymbol{\alpha}). \tag{5.23}$$

Genest *et al.* (1995) investigated the properties of this estimator and showed that it is consistent, asymptotically normal and fully efficient under independence. In addition to this, they showed by simulations that the method outperforms the method of moments for the bivariate Clayton copula.

5.2.3 The pseudo sample

When we have estimated the marginals, either parametrically or nonparametrically, we can plot the pseudo sample from the copula. The pseudo sample consists of the vectors $\widehat{U}_1, \ldots, \widehat{U}_n$, where

$$\widehat{U}_j = (\widehat{U}_{j,1}, \ldots, \widehat{U}_{j,d})' = (\widehat{F}_1(x_{j,1}), \ldots, \widehat{F}_d(x_{j,d}))'. \tag{5.24}$$

Since the distribution of $F_1(X_1), \ldots, F_d(X_d)$ is the copula of X, the transformed variables can be considered as realizations of the underlying copula, and contain all information on the dependence.

From equation 5.23 on the facing page it is clear that the semi-parametric approach estimates the copula parameters by maximize the loglikelihood on the pseudo sample. This is a reasonable approach, since the pseudo sample can be viewed as a realization of the underlying copula.

The transformation to uniform variables can sometimes make it easier to check for dependence. This is illustrated in figure 5.1 on the next page. Figure 5.1a and figure 5.1c, at the left, shows 1,000 realizations from a bivariate distribution with exponential marginals. Both scatterplots give the impression that the pairs are dependent, but this is only true for figure 5.1c. This can clearly be seen from figure 5.1b and figure 5.1d, at the right, which shows scatterplots of the pseudo samples. Figure 5.1b is a realization from the independence copula and figure 5.1d is the realization of the Gumbel copula, which we actually used to construct figure 5.1c.

A pseudo sample from real data is found in figure 5.2 on page 84. In this plot we have transformed the data (stock returns) by using the empirical distribution functions. Again, the resulting scatterplots can be considered as observations of the underlying (bivariate) copula. This figure is discussed in more detail in section 5.2.4.

For more on detecting dependence from the pseudo sample we refer to Genest and Boies (2003). They introduce a graphical procedure, named Kendall plots, which is used to detect dependence. The Kendall plot is a plot with similarities to the usual QQ-plots.

5.2.4 Estimating the Gaussian and the *t*-copulas

In example 3.1.9 on page 26 we calculated Spearman's ρ, Kendall's τ and the linear correlation on three indices. The data set consists of almost 14 years of daily log-return data for the Swiss Market Index (SMI), Standard & Poor 500 (SP) and FTSE100 (FTSE). We will now use the same data set to estimate the parameters of the Gaussian copula and the *t*-copula by the semi-parametric method described in section 5.2.2 on the preceding page.

In figure 5.2 on page 84 we see the pseudo sample from the data, and it is interesting to see the clustering in the upper right and lower left corners. This means that relatively large events tends to appear simultaneously. The

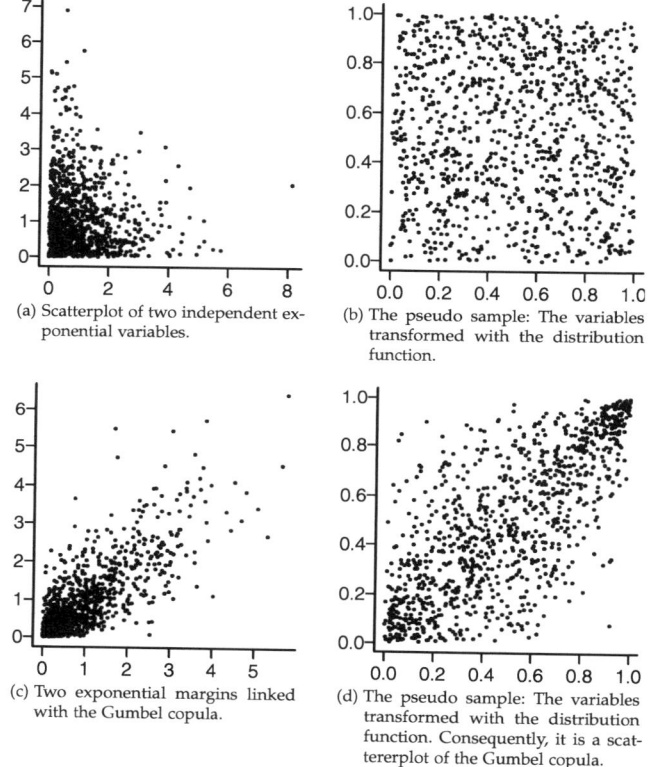

(a) Scatterplot of two independent exponential variables.

(b) The pseudo sample: The variables transformed with the distribution function.

(c) Two exponential margins linked with the Gumbel copula.

(d) The pseudo sample: The variables transformed with the distribution function. Consequently, it is a scattererplot of the Gumbel copula.

Figure 5.1: Figure (a) shows the scatterplot of 1,000 pairs of independent exponential random variables. This scatterplot makes the impression that the two variables are dependent, while figure (b), the corresponding pseudo sample, shows that they really are independent. Figure (c) shows two exponential marginals linked with the Gumbel copula. This scatterplot also makes the impression that they are dependent, and this is verified in (d). But from (d) we clearly see that the dependence increases in the upper tail.

appearance of simultaneous extreme events indicates that the t-copula will provide a better fit compared to the Gaussian copula. Moreover, if we compare figure 5.2 on the next page to simulated values from a bivariate t-copula, as in figure 4.2a on page 44, we see that they are very similar.

The normal copula: We used the semi-parametric approach to fit the Gaussian copula to the data. That is, we plugged the empirical distribution functions into the Gaussian copula and estimated the correlation matrix by maximum likelihood. The result can be found in table 5.3. The maximum value of the log-likelihood was 1,080. If we compare the estimated value of the correlation matrix with the sample values in table 3.1 on page 27, we see that the results are similar.

	FTSE	SMI	SP
FTSE	1.00	0.71	0.43
SMI	0.71	1.00	0.39
SP	0.43	0.39	1.00

Table 5.3: The correlation matrix in the Gaussian copula estimated by the semi-parametric approach.

The t-copula: We will now use the semi-parametric method to fit the t-copula to the same data set. We see in table 5.4 on page 85 that the estimated correlation matrix is very close to the one estimated for the normal copula. The degrees of freedom were estimated to be $\nu = 4.46 \approx 4$. The maximum value of the log-likelihood was 1,212, and compared to the log-likelihood of Gaussian copula, this is an increase by 132, which indicates a better fit. If we also compare the Akaike information criteria (AIC) to find the model that gives the best fit to the data with a minimum of parameters, we see that the t-copula gives a better fit. The AIC value for the t-copula is $-2,420$ and the AIC value for the Gaussian copula is $-2,158$. Remember that the one with the lowest AIC value is preferred. For more details about information criteria, see section 6.1 on page 88.

We have also used the relationship between Kendall's τ and the linear correlation, given in equation 5.9 on page 77, to estimate the correlation matrix. We see from tables 5.4 on page 85 and 5.5 on page 85 that the results from

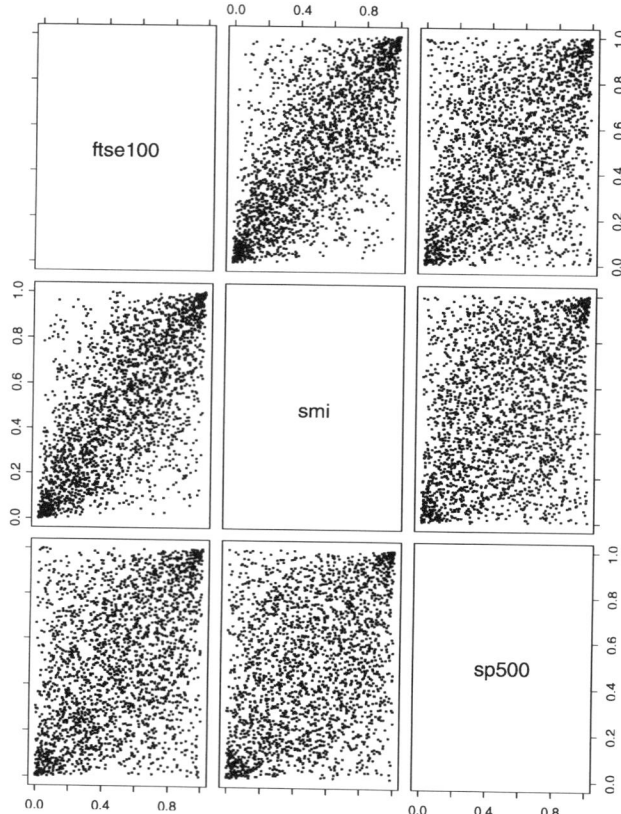

Figure 5.2: Pairwise scatterplots of the pseudo sample from Swiss Market Index, Standard & Poor 500 and FTSE100. The Pseudo sample is the original sample after we have transformed both variables using the empirical distribution function. This makes the random variables approximately uniform, and the association is easier to see; just look for clusters.

	FTSE	SMI	SP
FTSE	1.00	0.70	0.43
SMI	0.70	1.00	0.38
SP	0.43	0.38	1.00

Table 5.4: The correlation matrix for the t-copula estimated by maximum likelihood. See section 4.3 on page 41 and equation 2.9 on page 14 for the definition of the correlation matrix R for the t-copula.

the two methods are almost identical. If we were using the robust estimator of correlation based on Kendall's τ, the remaining parameter ν should be estimated by maximum likelihood.

	FTSE	SMI	SP
FTSE	1.00	0.70	0.43
SMI	0.70	1.00	0.37
SP	0.43	0.37	1.00

Table 5.5: The correlation matrix estimated by the relationship between Kendall's τ and the linear correlation in elliptical distributions. Consequently, this matrix should be a valid estimate for both the t and the Gaussian copula.

5.3 Non parametric modelling

In the discussion above we have assumed a specific parametric copula, and, sometimes, specific marginal distributions. In this section we will investigate a completely nonparametric method, where we obviously avoid the problem of choosing a reasonable copula. This gives us a completely objective estimation procedure which can be a good alternative if we have a fairly big amount of good data available.

5.3.1 The empirical copula

The empirical copula was, according to Nelsen (2006), first introduced by Deheuvels (1979), who called it the empirical dependence function. The empirical copulas are basically the multivariate empirical distribution functions, in other words, the observed frequency of $\mathbb{P}(U_1 < u_1, \ldots, U_d < u_d)$.

The empirical copula is given by

$$C_n(\boldsymbol{u}) = \frac{1}{n} \sum_{j=1}^{n} I\left\{ \widehat{F}_{n,1}(X_{j,1}) \leq u_1, \ldots, \widehat{F}_{n,d}(X_{j,d}) \leq u_d \right\} \tag{5.25}$$

$$= \frac{1}{n} \sum_{j=1}^{n} \prod_{i=1}^{d} I\left\{ \widehat{F}_{n,i}(X_{j,i}) \leq u_i \right\}, \tag{5.26}$$

where $\widehat{F}_{n,i}(X_{j,i})$ is the empirical distribution function given in equation 5.21 on page 80, and I is an indicator function (see equation 5.22 on page 80).

It is somewhat interesting to see that this can be expressed in terms of the ranks of the data. Let $R_{1,i}, \ldots, R_{n,i}$ be the ranks of the random variable X_i for $i = 1, \ldots, d$. Then we get that the empirical distribution function can be written

$$\widehat{F}_{n,i}(X_{j,i}) = \frac{R_{j,i}}{n+1}, \tag{5.27}$$

and consequently,

$$C_n(\boldsymbol{u}) = \frac{1}{n} \sum_{j=1}^{n} I\left\{ \frac{R_{j,1}}{n+1} \leq u_1, \ldots, \frac{R_{j,d}}{n+1} \leq u_d \right\} \tag{5.28}$$

$$= \frac{1}{n} \sum_{j=1}^{n} \prod_{i=1}^{d} I\left\{ \frac{R_{j,i}}{n+1} \leq u_i \right\}. \tag{5.29}$$

Since the empirical copula is a rank-based estimator of the unknown quantity $C(\boldsymbol{u})$, it plays a central role in goodness of fit procedures which we describe in more details in chapter 6. The empirical copula is also used by Genest and Rémillard (2004) to construct a test of independence.

6

Which copula is the right one?

In the previous chapter we looked at several methods of estimating the parameters in a specific copula. However, one question remains: Which copula is the right one? The possible combinations of the marginals and the copula are unlimited, so we need formal procedures to test the fit of the copula.

The simplest goodness of fit (GOF) test, would be a multidimensional chi-squared test. But difficulties arise since, in most situations, the marginal distributions are unknown and treated as nuisance parameters. The chi-square procedure does not work in general when replacing the marginal distributions by the estimated marginals (Fermanian 2005). For this reason there are no agreed upon method for selecting a copula model. However, there are several researchers working on this problem. The goal of this chapter is to summarize some of the research up to this date.

As in chapter 5, we let $X = (X_1, \ldots, X_d)'$ denote a generic random vector with multivariate distribution function F and continuous marginal distribution functions $F_1, \ldots, F_d$. In addition we assume that we have n independent copies of X, denoted $X_1, \ldots, X_n$, where $X_j = (X_{j,1}, \ldots, X_{j,d})'$ for $j = 1, \ldots, n$ is an individual data vector.

6.1 Information criteria

After having estimated several copula models with maximum likelihood, we need to choose the best one. Since our models are in general not nested[1] we can not use a likelihood ratio test. But if we can assume that the true model is among the estimated models, the simplest procedure is to choose the model with the lowest value of the Akaike or Bayes information criteria, abbreviated AIC or BIC, respectively.

Consider a sample of size n. Let the number of parameters (θ, α) in our estimated model equal to q, and let $l(\widehat{\theta}, \widehat{\alpha})$ denote the value of the maximized log-likelihood. The AIC and the BIC are then given by

$$\text{AIC} = -2l(\widehat{\theta}, \widehat{\alpha}) + 2q \tag{6.1}$$

and

$$\text{BIC} = -2l(\widehat{\theta}, \widehat{\alpha}) + q\ln(n). \tag{6.2}$$

We compute the AIC or BIC for each model, and select the model with the smallest value of the information criteria. We see that these criteria compare the value of the likelihoods while penalizing overfitting.

For more on AIC and BIC see Burnham and Anderson (2004) and the references therein. For an application of this method in a copula setting see Breymann et al. (2003).

6.2 Goodness of fit procedures

Several authors are working on goodness of fit procedures for copula models. Breymann et al. (2003) propose a test based on the Rosenblatt transformation by Rosenblatt (1952) (theorem 6.2.1 on the facing page), Chen et al. (2004) propose two tests: first, a test based on the kernel density estimator; second, an approach similar to the test by Breymann et al. (2003). Berg and Bakken (2007) is working to improve the test by Breymann et al. (2003) and propose another test based on the Rosenblatt transformation. And finally, Genest et al. (2006a) propose a GOF test based on the empirical copula.

In this section we will briefly review the main results of these different approaches.

---

[1]Two models are nested if one is a special case of the other model with constraints on the parameter values.

6.2.1 The Rosenblatt transformation

As mentioned above, Breymann *et al.* (2003), Chen *et al.* (2004) and Berg and Bakken (2007) provides different GOF tests for copula models based on the Rosenblatt transformation. The Rosenblatt transformation transforms a set of dependent variables into a set of independent uniformly distributed variables. The transformation is defined as follows:

Theorem 6.2.1: The Rosenblatt transformation

Let $X = (X_1, \ldots, X_d)'$ be a random vector with distribution function F. Let $z_i = T_i(x_1, \ldots, x_i)$, where T is the transformation given by

$$z_1 = T_1(x_1) = \mathbb{P}(X_1 \leq x_1) = F_{X_1}(x_1), \tag{6.3}$$
$$z_2 = T_2(x_1, x_2) = \mathbb{P}(X_2 \leq x_2 \mid X_1 = x_1) = F_{X_2|X_1}(x_2 \mid x_1), \tag{6.4}$$
$$\vdots \tag{6.5}$$
$$z_d = T_d(x_1, \ldots, x_d) = \mathbb{P}(X_d \leq x_d \mid X_1 = x_1, \ldots, X_{d-1} = x_{d-1}) \tag{6.6}$$
$$= F_{X_d|X_1,\ldots,X_{d-1}}(x_d \mid x_1, \ldots, x_{d-1}). \tag{6.7}$$

Then the random variables $Z_i = T(X_1, \ldots, X_i)$, for $i = 1, \ldots, d$, are uniformly and independently distributed on $[0, 1]^d$. In other words, Z_i are mutually independent and uniformly distributed on $[0, 1]$.

Proof: See Rosenblatt (1952).

A consequence of the Rosenblatt transformation is that X has distribution function F if and only if the distribution of the transformed variables Z is

$$F(z_1, \ldots, z_d) = \prod_{i=1}^{d} z_i. \tag{6.8}$$

From this we can test whether the data vectors $X_1, \ldots, X_n$ are a realization of a population with distribution function F by testing whether $Z_1, \ldots, Z_n$ is a sample from a population uniformly distributed on $(0, 1)^d$. For details, see Rosenblatt (1952).

This procedure can be generalized to a copula setting. Assume that C is the copula of F such that

$$F(\boldsymbol{x}) = C(F_1(x_1), \ldots, F_d(x_d)) \qquad (6.9)$$
$$= C(u_1, \ldots, u_d). \qquad (6.10)$$

Let

$$C_i(u_1, \ldots, u_i) = C(u_1, \ldots, u_i, 1, \ldots, 1), \quad \text{for } i = 1, \ldots, d, \qquad (6.11)$$

denote the i-dimensional marginal distribution. Remark that $C_1(u_1) = u_1$ and $C_d(\boldsymbol{u}) = C(\boldsymbol{u})$. Then the Rosenblatt transformation of the copula data $(u_1, \ldots, u_d) = (F_1(x_1), \ldots, F_d(x_d))$ becomes,

$$z_1 = u_1, \qquad (6.12)$$

and

$$z_i = C_i(u_i \mid u_1, \ldots, u_{i-1}) \qquad (6.13)$$
$$= \frac{\partial^{i-1} C_i(u_1, \ldots, u_i)}{\partial u_1 \cdots \partial u_{i-1}} \bigg/ \frac{\partial^{i-1} C_{i-1}(u_1, \ldots, u_{i-1})}{\partial u_1 \cdots \partial u_{i-1}}, \text{ for } i = 2, \ldots, d. \qquad (6.14)$$

Consequently, to test whether C is the distribution of $F_1, \ldots, F_d$ is equivalent to test whether

$$F(z_1, \ldots, z_d) = \prod_{i=1}^{d} z_i = \Pi(z_1, \ldots, z_d). \qquad (6.15)$$

Breymann, Dias and Embrechts' approach

The marginal distributions are usually unknown and Breymann *et al.* (2003) performs the Rosenblatt transformation on the pseudo sample of the copula of X. Let $X_1, \ldots, X_n$ be n realizations of X, where $X_j = (X_{j,1}, \ldots, X_{j,d})'$ for $j = 1, \ldots, n$ is an individual data vector. The pseudo sample is then given by,

$$\widehat{U}_j = (\widehat{U}_{j,1}, \ldots, \widehat{U}_{j,d})' = (\widehat{F}_1(x_{j,1}), \ldots, \widehat{F}_d(x_{j,d}))', \qquad (6.16)$$

where $\widehat{F}_i(x_{j,i})$, in Breymann *et al.* (2003), is the empirical distribution function. In addition to this, the parameters in the copula is usually estimated. Consequently,

$$\widehat{Z}_{j,1} = \widehat{F}_1(x_{j,1}), \qquad (6.17)$$

and
$$\widehat{Z}_{j,i} = C_i(\widehat{F}_i(X_{j,i}); \widehat{\alpha} \mid \widehat{F}_1(X_{j,1}), \dots, \widehat{F}_{i-1}(X_{j,i-1})), \quad \text{for } i = 2, \dots, d, \qquad (6.18)$$

where $\widehat{\alpha}$ is the estimated parameters of the copula. From this we get that

$$\widehat{S}_j = \sum_{i=1}^{d} (\Phi^{-1}(\widehat{Z}_{j,i}))^2, \quad \text{for } j = 1, \dots, n, \qquad (6.19)$$

is approximately chi-squared distributed with d degrees of freedom. By testing whether S_j for $j = 1, \dots, n$ has the required chi-square distribution, we can reject or accept the hypothesis that $U \sim C$. But, it is not quite clear how the empirical marginal distribution functions and the estimation of the parameters of the copula affects the finite sample distribution of S_j. To avoid this problem, several authors suggests using a parametric bootstrap procedure.

Berg and Bakken's approach

Chen *et al.* (2004) and Berg and Bakken (2007) points out that the test by Breymann *et al.* (2003) is not consistent. A test is consistent if the probability of rejecting the null-hypothesis when the null-hypothesis is wrong tends to one as n tends to infinity; in other words, a consistent test does not neglect deviations from the null hypothesis when the sample size tends to infinity. Berg and Bakken (2007) tried to improve the test by introducing two more transformations. First, they apply the Rosenblatt transformation on the copula data to obtain $Z = (Z_1, \dots, Z_d)'$ – mutually independent random variables with identical uniform distribution on $(0, 1)$ – and then they rearrange the Zs in increasing order,

$$Z_{(1)} \leq Z_{(2)} \cdots \leq Z_{(d)}, \qquad (6.20)$$

to obtain the (dependent) order statistics. Finally, they apply the Rosenblatt transformation on the order statistics to make them mutually independent and uniformly distributed on $(0, 1)$.

From the Markov property of order statistics,

$$F_{Z_{(i)}|Z_{(1)}, \dots, Z_{(i-1)}}(z_{(i)}) = F_{Z_{(i)}|Z_{(i-1)}}(z_{(i)}) \qquad (6.21)$$

and from Deheuvels (1984, Theorem 1)[2] they derive a simple expression for the Rosenblatt transformation on the order statistics of Z (recall that $F_{Z_i}(z_i) = z_i$):

$$h_i = T_i(z_{(i-1)}, z_{(i)}) = F_{Z_{(i)}|Z_{(i-1)}}(z_{(i)}) = 1 - \left(\frac{1 - z_{(i)}}{1 - z_{(i-1)}}\right)^{d-(i-1)}, \tag{6.22}$$

for $i = 1, \ldots, d$ and $z_{(0)} = 0$. From theorem 6.2.1 on page 89 we have that the new random variables $H_i = T(Z_{(i)}, Z_{(i-1)})$ for $i = 1, \ldots, d$ are mutually independent and $U(0, 1)$ distributed.

From this step they perform a dimension reduction, corresponding to equation 6.19 on the preceding page, based on Z and H:

$$S_j = \sum_{i=1}^{d} \Gamma_Z(Z_i)\Gamma_H(H_i), \tag{6.23}$$

where Γ_Z and Γ_H are weight functions used for weighting the information in Z and H, respectively. By choosing $\Gamma_Z = \Phi^{-1}(Z_i)^2$ and $\Gamma_H = 1$, we see that we get the same chi-squared distributed test statistics as in equation 6.19 on the previous page. In addition to this they suggests the following weighting functions for Z and H:

1. $\Phi^{-1}(X)$
2. $|X - 0.5|$
3. $(X - 0.5)^{\beta}$ for $\beta = 2, 4, \ldots$

From this step they suggest using a parametric bootstrap to estimate the distribution of S_j and then perform a test to see if S_j has the required distribution.

Chen, Fan and Patton's approach

Chen *et al.* (2004) suggests two approaches, one based on the Rosenblatt transformation and the kernel density estimator of the transformed data, and one based only on the Rosenblatt transformation. The latter is only a slight modification of the approach in Breymann *et al.* (2003), and will not be described here.

Let $X = (X_1, \ldots, X_d)'$ be a d-dimensional random vector. Under the hypothesis that the data are realizations of the distribution function F with copula C,

---

[2]See Deheuvels (1985) for a correction.

$Z = (Z_1, \ldots, Z_d)$, obtained from the Rosenblatt transformation of the pseudo sample, are i.i.d. $U(0,1)^d$. Consequently, if f_Z is the density of F_Z, then

$$f_Z(z) = 1, \quad \text{if } U \sim C. \tag{6.24}$$

To test this hypothesis Chen *et al.* (2004) uses a kernel estimator $\bar{f}_Z(z)$ of $f_Z(z)$,

$$\bar{f}_Z(z) = \frac{1}{nh^d} \sum_{j=1}^{n} \left(\prod_{i=1}^{d} K_h(z_i, Z_{j,i}) \right), \tag{6.25}$$

and looks at the distance between the kernel estimator and the assumed density of Z as follows.

$$\bar{I}_n = \int_0^1 \cdots \int_0^1 (\bar{f}_Z(z) - f_Z(z))^2 \, dz_1 \ldots dz_d \tag{6.26}$$

$$= \int_0^1 \cdots \int_0^1 (\bar{f}_Z(z) - 1)^2 \, dz_1 \ldots dz_d. \tag{6.27}$$

There also exists other functionals measuring the distance between two densities, and perhaps a different distance function would be more appropriate; see Skaug and Tjøstheim (1996).

Unfortunately, we can not observe Z_i directly, and Chen *et al.* (2004) compute the pseudo observations of Z by estimating the marginals by the empirical marginal distribution as in equation 6.17 on page 90. From this they base the test on

$$\hat{I}_n = \int_0^1 \cdots \int_0^1 (\hat{f}_Z(z) - 1) \, dz_1 \ldots dz_d, \tag{6.28}$$

where $\hat{f}_Z(z)$ is the kernel estimator of $f_Z(z)$ constructed from the pseudo observations $\hat{Z}$. In addition to this, Chen *et al.* (2004) shows that under certain conditions the asymptotic distribution of $\hat{I}_n$ is the same as the asymptotic distribution of $\bar{I}_n$.

As the authors point out, procedures based on kernel estimators will not perform well when the dimension d is large, say $d \geq 4$, because of the curse of dimensionality. In these situations Chen *et al.* (2004) suggests to use the test by Breymann *et al.* (2003).

6.2.2 Tests based on the empirical copula

To test the hypothesis that the distribution of X is F, or equivalent, that the distribution of $F_1, \ldots, F_d$ is given by the copula C, it is very natural to look at the empirical copula. The empirical copula is given by

$$C_n(u) = \frac{1}{n} \sum_{j=1}^{n} I\left\{ \widehat{F}_{n,1}(X_{j,1}) \le u_1, \ldots, \widehat{F}_{n,d}(X_{j,d}) \le u_d \right\} \tag{6.29}$$

$$= \frac{1}{n} \sum_{j=1}^{n} \prod_{i=1}^{d} I\left\{ \widehat{F}_{n,i}(X_{j,i}) \le u_i \right\}, \tag{6.30}$$

where $\widehat{F}_{n,i}(X_{j,i})$ is the empirical distribution function given in equation 5.21 on page 80, and I is an indicator function (see equation 5.22 on page 80). C_n is a non-parametric estimator of the underlying copula C, and the goodness of fit tests is based on comparing the distance between C_n and $C_{\widehat{\alpha}}$.

The Cramer von Mises and the Kolmogorov-Smirnov statistics based on the empirical copula becomes

$$S_n = n \int_{[0,1]^d} \left\{ C_n(u) - C_{\widehat{\alpha}}(u) \right\}^2 dC_n(u) \tag{6.31}$$

$$= \sum_{j=1}^{n} \left\{ C_n(\widehat{F}_{j,1}(x_{j,1}), \ldots, \widehat{F}_{j,d}(x_{j,d})) - C_{\widehat{\alpha}}(\widehat{F}_{j,1}(x_{j,1}), \ldots, \widehat{F}_{j,d}(x_{j,d})) \right\}^2, \tag{6.32}$$

and

$$T_n = \sup_{u \in [0,1]^d} \sqrt{n} |C_n(u) - C_{\widehat{\alpha}}(u)|, \tag{6.33}$$

respectively. Large values of either one lead to the rejection of the null-hypothesis.

Since both of the statistics depends on the parameters in the copula α we need to approximate P-values for these tests by a parametric bootstrap procedure. This procedure is further described in Genest *et al.* (2006b) and the references therein.

7

Credit risk models

There are two main applications of credit risk models: risk management, and pricing of securities exposed to credit risk. In risk management the goal is to determine the loss distribution of a financial portfolio exposed to credit risk. Since the loss distribution is given for a fixed time period, these models are usually static. In the credit risk valuation problem, on the other hand, the price may depend on the exact time of default; thus we need a dynamic model to price these securities. These are typically continuous time models.

Furthermore, credit risk models are usually divided into structural models and reduced form models. In structural models the mechanism leading to a default is specified. It will typically be when the value of the assets falls below the value of the liabilities. Therefore, a default occurs whenever a stochastic variable or a stochastic process representing assets falls below a threshold representing liabilities. A well known example of a structural model is Merton's model for risky bonds (Merton 1974).

In reduced form models, on the other hand, we do not specify the mechanism leading to a default. Instead we model the time until default as a stochastic variable, or a stochastic process, depending on common economic variables.

An extensive theory based on (multivariate) Brownian motions has been developed to build credit risk models. Since our focus is on copulas, we will only present copula models.

This chapter is for the most part based on McNeil *et al.* (2005, chapter 8). More references will be given in the text.

7.1 Static models

Stochastic processes are used to describe the evolution of risk in time in financial mathematics. If we turn our focus to risk management, our goal is to determine the loss distribution over a *fixed* time period. A stochastic process is then reduced to a stochastic variable and several stochastic processes are reduced to a stochastic vector.

In the static setting we are free to use copulas to describe the dependence between the risk factors. This is valuable, since it is easier to specify the marginal default probability than the dependence between them. The marginal default probability can be obtained from historical default information from rating agencies, it can be calculated from a theoretical model or we can use information available from market prices of defaultable bonds or credit derivatives. When we have specified the marginal default probability we can use copulas to investigate the impact of different dependence structures.

7.1.1 Multivariate static structural models and copulas

In a one-period $[0, T]$ structural model default occurs when a random variable X, usually representing the values of the company, lies below a given threshold d at time T.

We will now expand this to a multivariate setting. Assume that we have m companies. Let $X = (X_1, \ldots, X_m)'$ be the vector that describes the mechanism leading to a default and let $d = (d_1, \ldots, d_m)'$ be the vector of thresholds. Consequently, default for company i occurs if $X_i < d_i$. Typically the multivariate normal or lognormal distribution are used to model the distribution of X, but, in this very general setting, we are allowed to assume any multivariate distribution for X.

In addition to this we introduce the default indicator Y_i as

$$Y_i = \begin{cases} 1 & \text{if } X_i \leq d_i; \\ 0 & \text{if } X_i > d_i. \end{cases} \qquad (7.1)$$

The joint probability function will be denoted $f(y) = \mathbb{P}(Y_1 = y_1, \ldots, Y_m = y_m)$, $y \in \{0,1\}^m$ and the marginal default probabilities will be $\bar{p}_i = \mathbb{P}(Y_i = 1)$. We also count the number of defaults at time T by the random variable $N = \sum_{i=1}^m Y_i$.

Since

$$\text{Var}(Y_i) = \mathbb{E}(Y_i^2) - \mathbb{E}(Y_i)^2 \qquad (7.2)$$
$$= \mathbb{E}(Y_i) - \bar{p}_i^2 \qquad (7.3)$$
$$= \bar{p}_i - \bar{p}_i^2, \qquad (7.4)$$

we obtain the pairwise default correlation

$$\rho(Y_i, Y_j) = \frac{\mathbb{E}(Y_i Y_j) - \bar{p}_i \bar{p}_j}{\sqrt{(\bar{p}_i - \bar{p}_i^2)(\bar{p}_j - \bar{p}_j^2)}}, \quad \text{for } i \neq j. \qquad (7.5)$$

Since $\mathbb{E}(Y_i Y_j) = \mathbb{P}(X_i \leq d_i, X_j \leq d_j)$ the default correlation is determined by the joint distribution of X, but note that the default correlation is in general different from the correlation between the assets.

Industry models

The widely used credit risk models CreditMetrics^{TM} and KMV are in principle identical. The main difference is in how they calibrate the model to real world problems, a problem which we do not describe in this chapter.

In both models X is assumed to have a multivariate normal distribution and X_i is interpreted as the change in asset value. Moreover, d_i is chosen such that it matches the given default probability $\bar{p}_i$ for company i.

Extension of Merton's model

In Merton's model the asset values X_t, now a stochastic process depending on time, is assumed to follow a geometric Brownian motion given by

$$dX_t = \mu_X X_t \, dt + \sigma_X X_t \, dW_t, \tag{7.6}$$

$$X_0 = x > 0, \tag{7.7}$$

for constants $\mu_X \in \mathbb{R}$ and $\sigma_X > 0$ and a Brownian motion W_t. This stochastic differential equation is solved by standard tools from financial mathematics. It is given by

$$X_T = X_0 e^{(\mu_X - \frac{1}{2}\sigma_X^2)T + \sigma_X W_T}, \tag{7.8}$$

which implies that X_T, at a given time T, is lognormally distributed, or, equivalent, that

$$\ln X_T \sim N(\ln X_0 + (\mu_X - \frac{1}{2}\sigma_X^2)T, \sigma_X^2 T). \tag{7.9}$$

From this we get that the (physical) default probability of the firm is

$$\mathbb{P}(X_T \leq d) = \mathbb{P}(\ln X_t \leq \ln d) = \Phi\left(\frac{\ln(\frac{d}{X_0}) - (\mu_X - \frac{1}{2}\sigma_X^2)T}{\sigma_X \sqrt{T}}\right). \tag{7.10}$$

Moreover, under some assumptions, among them that X_t is a traded security with dynamics given by equation 7.6, we have that the risk neutral default probability is given by

$$\mathbb{P}(X_T \leq d) = \Phi\left(\frac{\ln(\frac{d}{X_0}) - (r - \frac{1}{2}\sigma_X^2)T}{\sigma_X \sqrt{T}}\right), \tag{7.11}$$

where r is a constant deterministic short rate.

It is possible to generalize this model to a multivariate framework by using the theory of higher dimensional stochastic calculus, but this is outside the scope of this text. It will result in a model where the value of X_T at a given time T follows a multivariate normal distribution. To avoid this we follow Cherubini et al. (2004). He uses copulas to specify the multivariate distributions.

Consider m companies with asset values given by $X_t = (X_{t,1}, \ldots, X_{t,m})'$, where $X_{t,i}$, for $i = 1, \ldots, m$, follows independent one-dimensional geometric Brownian motions. Let, as before, the vector of thresholds be given by $d =$

$(d_1, \ldots, d_m)'$. Then the risk neutral default probability of the ith company is given by

$$\mathbb{P}(X_{T,i} \leq d_i) = \Phi\left(\frac{\ln(\frac{d_i}{X_{0,i}}) - (r - \frac{1}{2}\sigma_{X_i}^2)T}{\sigma_{X_i}\sqrt{T}}\right) \qquad (7.12)$$

$$= \Phi(\xi_{T,i}). \qquad (7.13)$$

According to Sklar's theorem the joint default probability can always be written

$$\mathbb{P}(X_{T,1} \leq d_1, \ldots, X_{T,m} \leq d_m) = C(\Phi(\xi_{T,1}), \ldots, \Phi(\xi_{T,m})), \qquad (7.14)$$

and we can use any multivariate copula to describe the dependence between defaults.

As an example, consider two firms with debt $d_1 = 0.5$ and $d_2 = 0.7$, and asset values $X_{0,1} = X_{0,2} = 1$. Assume that $\sigma_{X_1} = \sigma_{X_2} = 0.2$, that the short rate $r = 0$ and that $T = 5$. From equation 7.12 we get that $\mathbb{P}(X_{T,1} \leq d_1) = 0.0606$ and $\mathbb{P}(X_{T,2} \leq d_2) = 0.2126$. Consequently, the joint default probability will be $C(0.0606, 0.2126)$. From this point it is interesting to investigate the effect of different copulas on the joint default probability. An obvious starting point is to calculate the upper and lower bound of the joint default probability. From the Fréchet copulas (equation 4.69 on page 59) we get that the joint default probability always will stay between $W(\Phi(\xi_{T,1}), \Phi(\xi_{T,2})) = 0$ and $M(\Phi(\xi_{T,1}), \Phi(\xi_{T,2})) = 0.0606$.

7.1.2 Survival times

Li (2001) introduced dependence between the 'time until default' by using copulas.

Let the life time of company i be represented by the stochastic variable T_i with distribution function

$$F_i(t) = \mathbb{P}(T_i \leq t), \quad t \geq 0, \qquad (7.15)$$

and survival function

$$\overline{F_i}(t) = \mathbb{P}(T_i > t) = 1 - F_i(t), \quad t \geq 0. \qquad (7.16)$$

We assume that F_i is absolute continuous and denote the density function by

$$f_i(t) = \frac{\mathrm{d}}{\mathrm{d}t} F_i(t) = -\frac{\mathrm{d}}{\mathrm{d}t} \overline{F}_i(t), \tag{7.17}$$

and the hazard rate at age t as

$$\mu_i(t) = \frac{\mathrm{d}}{\mathrm{d}t}(-\ln \overline{F}_i(t)) = \frac{f_i(t)}{1 - F_i(t)}. \tag{7.18}$$

The hazard rate function $\mu_i(t)$ can be interpreted as the instantaneous default probability for a security that has attained age t.

Integrating equation 7.18 from 0 to t and using $\overline{F}_i(0) = 0$, we obtain

$$\overline{F}_i(t) = e^{-\int_0^t \mu_i(s)\,\mathrm{d}s}. \tag{7.19}$$

Obviously, company i defaults by time T if $T_i \leq T$, so the default probability is $F_i(T)$. If we know, or assume we know, the marginal default probabilities, we can use any copula to determine the multivariate distribution of $\boldsymbol{T} = (T_1, \ldots, T_m)'$ such that,

$$F_{\boldsymbol{T}}(t_1, \ldots, t_m) = C(F_1(t_1), \ldots, F_m(t_m)) \tag{7.20}$$

$$= C(1 - e^{-\int_0^t \mu_1(s)\,\mathrm{d}s}, \ldots, 1 - e^{-\int_0^t \mu_m(s)\,\mathrm{d}s}). \tag{7.21}$$

Li assumes that the hazard rate is constant, so that $\mu_i(t) = \lambda_i$. This leads us to the well-known exponential distribution

$$F_i(t) = 1 - e^{-\lambda_i t}. \tag{7.22}$$

Li also assumes that $\boldsymbol{T} = (T_1, \ldots, T_m)'$ has a Gaussian copula $C_{\boldsymbol{R}}^{\mathrm{GA}}$ for some correlation matrix $\boldsymbol{R}$.

Li's assumptions leads to a meta-Gaussian distribution with exponential margins as in figure 4.1d on page 42. Obviously, any copula can be used to determine the joint distribution function of the default times. In figure 5.1c on page 82 we see the meta Gumbel distribution with exponential margins. These plots can be viewed as 1,500 simulated survival times for two companies with marginal density function $f(t) = e^{-t}$, but different dependence structure.

Appendix

A.1 The gamma and the inverse gamma distribution

Note that the random variable Y has a gamma distribution $Y \sim \Gamma(\alpha, \beta)$ if its density is given by

$$f(y) = \frac{\beta^\alpha}{\Gamma(\alpha)} y^{\alpha-1} e^{-\beta y}, \quad y > 0, \quad \alpha > 0, \quad \beta > 0. \tag{A.1}$$

If $X = \frac{1}{Y}$, then X has an inverse gamma distribution $X \sim IG(\alpha, \beta)$ and its density is given by

$$f(x) = \frac{\beta^\alpha}{\Gamma(\alpha)} x^{-(\alpha+1)} e^{-\frac{\beta}{x}}, \quad x > 0, \quad \alpha > 0, \quad \beta > 0. \tag{A.2}$$

A.2 Symmetry

We say that a random variable X is symmetric about a if $\mathbb{P}(X - a \leq x) = \mathbb{P}(a - X \leq x)$. When X is continuous we get that

$$F(a + x) = \bar{F}(a - x). \tag{A.3}$$

101

Definition A.2.1: Bivariate symmetry

Let X_1 and X_2 be random variables and let (a, b) be a point in $\mathbb{R}^2$.

1. (X_1, X_2) is marginally symmetric about (a, b) if X_1 and X_2 are symmetric about a and b, respectively.
2. (X_1, X_2) is radially symmetric about (a, b) if the joint distribution function of $X_1 - a$ and $X_2 - b$ is the same as the joint distribution for $a - X_1$ and $b - X_2$.

If X_1 and X_2 are continuous, we can express the condition for marginal and radial symmetry tn terms of the distribution functions.

Theorem A.2.2

Let X_1 and X_2 be continuous random variables with joint distribution function F and margins F_1 and F_2. Let (a, b) be a point in $\mathbb{R}^2$. Then (X_1, X_2) is radially symmetric about a if and only if

$$F(a + x_1, b + x_2) = \bar{F}(a - x_1, b - x_2) \quad \forall (x_1, x_2) \in \mathbb{R}^2. \qquad \text{(A.4)}$$

For further details see Nelsen (2006, pages 36–38).

Definition A.2.3: Radial symmetry $n \geq 2$

A random vector X is radially symmetric about a if

$$X - a \overset{D}{=} a - X, \qquad \text{(A.5)}$$

where $\overset{D}{=}$ means equal in distribution.

A.3 Exchangeability

Consider a random vector $X = (X_1, \ldots, X_n)'$. If the subscripts, the 'labels' identifying the random variables, are uninformative such that the information from x_i's is independent from the order in which they are collected, then the sequence of random variables are said to be exchangeable. Consequently, we can reorder the random vector in any way without affecting the joint distribution.

Definition A.3.1: Exchangeability

A random vector X is exchangeable if

$$(X_1, \ldots, X_n) \overset{d}{=} (X_{\pi(1)}, \ldots, X_{\pi(n)}) \tag{A.6}$$

for all permutations of $\pi(1), \ldots, \pi(n)$ defined on $(1, \ldots, n)$.

A.4 Copula densities

The density of a absolutely continuous copula is given by

$$c(u_1, \ldots, u_n) = \frac{\partial C(u_1, \ldots, u_n)}{\partial u_1, \ldots, \partial u_n}. \tag{A.7}$$

According to McNeil *et al.* (2005, page 197) all the *parametric* copulas we have met in this thesis have densities given by equation A.7.

For an implicit copula of an absolutely continuous joint distribution function F with strictly increasing, continuous marginals $F_1, \ldots, F_n$ we get that the copula density is given by

$$c(u_1, \ldots, u_n) = \frac{f(F_1^{-1}(u_1), \ldots, F_n^{-1}(u_n))}{f_1(F_1^{-1}(u_1)) \ldots f_n(F_n^{-1}(u_n))}, \tag{A.8}$$

where f is the joint density of F and $f_1, \ldots, f_n$ are the univariate densities of the marginal distributions $F_1, \ldots, F_n$.

A.5 Conditional copulas

Conditional copulas are heavily related to parial derivatives. Since the copula is an increasing (lemma 4.1.5) continuous (lemma 4.1.6) function in each argument we have that

$$C_{U_1|U_1}(u_2 \mid u_1) = \mathbb{P}(U_2 \leq u_2 \mid U_1 = u_1) \tag{A.9}$$

$$= \lim_{\delta \to 0} \frac{C(u_1 + \delta, u_2) - C(u_1, u_2)}{\delta} \tag{A.10}$$

$$= \frac{\partial}{\partial u_1} C(u_1, u_2). \tag{A.11}$$

$$C_{U_1|U_1}(u_2 \mid u_1) = \mathbb{P}(U_2 \leq u_2 \mid U_1 = u_1) = \lim_{\delta \to 0} \frac{C(u_1 + \delta, u_2) - C(u_1, u_2)}{\delta}$$

$$\text{(A.12)}$$

$$= \frac{\partial}{\partial u_1} C(u_1, u_2). \qquad \text{(A.13)}$$

See Nelsen (2006, therem 2.2.7) for the existence of the partial derivatives of a copula.

Bibliography

Berg D. and Bakken H. (2007). 'A goodness-of-fit test for copulae based on the conditional probability integral transform'. Cited on pages 88, 89 and 91.

Bingham N. and Kiesel R. (2002). 'Semi-parametric modelling in finance: theoretical foundations'. *Quantitative Finance*, **volume 2**, no. 4, pages 241–250. DOI: 10.1088/1469-7688/2/4/201. Cited on page 12.

Breymann W., Dias A. and Embrechts P. (2003). 'Dependence structures for multivariate high-frequency data in finance'. *Quantitative Finance*, **volume 3**, no. 1, pages 1–14. Cited on pages 88, 89, 90, 91, 92 and 93.

Burnham K. and Anderson D. (2004). 'Multimodel inference: Understanding AIC and BIC in model selection'. *Sociological Methods & Research*, **volume 33**, no. 2, pages 261–304. DOI: 10.1177/0049124104268644. Cited on page 88.

Campbell J., Lo A. and MacKinley A. (1997). *Financial Econometrics*. Princeton University Press. Cited on page 8.

Casella G. and Berger R.L. (2002). *Statistical Inference*. Duxbury Press. Cited on page 13.

Chavez-Demoulin V. and Roehrl (2004). 'Extreme value theory can save your neck'. Cited on page 19.

Chen X., Fan Y. and Patton A. (2004). 'Simple tests for models of dependence between multiple financial time series, with applications to US equity returns and exchange rates'. Financial Markets Group, London School of Economics, Discussion paper 483. Cited on pages 88, 89, 91, 92 and 93.

Cherubini U., Luciano E. and Vecchiato W. (2004). *Copula methods in finance*. John Wiley & Sons Ltd. ISBN 0-470-86344-7. Cited on page 98.

Clayton D.G. (1978). 'A model for association in bivariate life tables and its application in epidemiological studies of familial tendency in chronic disease incidence'. *Biometrika*, **volume 65**, pages 141–151. DOI: 10.1093/biomet/65.1.141. Cited on page 50.

Deheuvels P. (1979). 'La fonction de dépendance empirique et ses propriétés, un test non paramétrique d'indépendance'. *Bulletin de l'Académie Royal de Belgique, Classe des Sciences*, **volume 65**, pages 274–292. Cited on page 85.

Deheuvels P. (1984). 'The characterization of distributions by order statistics and record values: A unified approach'. *Journal of Applied Probability*, **volume 21**, no. 2, pages 326–334. DOI: 10.2307/3213643. Cited on page 92.

Deheuvels P. (1985). 'Correction: The characterization of distributions by order statistics and record values: A unified approach'. *Journal of Applied Probability*, **volume 22**, no. 4, page 997. DOI: 10.2307/3213972. Cited on page 92.

Demarta S. and McNeil A. (2005). 'The t copula and related copulas'. *International Statistical Review*, **volume 73**, no. 1, pages 111–129. URL: http://www.blackwell-synergy.com/doi/abs/10.1111/j.1751-5823.2005.tb00254.x. Cited on page 43.

Eberlein E. and Keller U. (1995). 'Hyperbolic distributions in finance'. *Bernoulli*, **volume 1**, pages 281–299. DOI: 10.2307/3318481. Cited on page 12.

Embrechts P., C. K. and Mikosch D. (1997). *Modelling Extremal Events for Insurance and Finance*. Springer. Cited on pages 16, 17 and 19.

Embrechts P., Lindskog F. and McNeil A. (2001). 'Modelling dependence with copulas'. *Technical report*. Cited on pages 34 and 45.

Embrechts P., McNeil A. and Straumann D. (2002). 'Correlation and dependency in risk management: Properties and pitfalls'. In Dempster M. (editor), 'Risk Management: Value at Risk and Beyond', pages 176–223. Cambridge University Press. Cited on pages 8, 23 and 67.

Fermanian J. (2005). 'Goodness-of-fit tests for copulas'. *Journal of Multivariate Analysis*, **volume 95**, no. 1, pages 119–152. DOI: 10.1016/j.jmva.2004.07.004. Cited on page 87.

Frahm G., Junker M. and Schmidt R. (2005). 'Estimating the tail-dependence coefficient: Properties and pitfalls'. *Insurance: Mathematics and Economics*, **volume 37**, no. 1, pages 80–100. ISSN 0167-6687. DOI: 10.1016/j.insmatheco.2005.05.008. Cited on page 32.

Frees E. and Valdez E. (1998). 'Understanding relationships using copulas'. *North American Actuarial Journal*, **volume 2**, no. 1, pages 1–25. URL: http://www.soa.org/files/pdf/naaj9801_1.pdf. Cited on page 63.

Genest C. (1987). 'Frank's family of bivariate distributions'. *Biometrika*, **volume 74**, no. 3, pages 549–555. DOI: 10.1093/biomet/74.3.549. Cited on page 49.

Genest C. and Boies J. (2003). 'Detecting dependence with Kendall plots.' *The American Statistician*, **volume 57**, no. 4, pages 275–285. Cited on page 81.

Genest C., Ghoudi K. and Rivest L. (1995). 'A semi-parametric estimation procedure of dependence parameters in multivariate families of distributions'. *Biometrika*, **volume 82**, pages 543–552. DOI: 10.1093/biomet/82.3.543. Cited on page 80.

Genest C. and MacKay J. (1986). 'The joy of copulas: Bivariate distributions with uniform marginals'. *The American Statistician*, **volume 40**, no. 4, pages 280–283. DOI: 10.2307/2684602. Cited on page 63.

Genest C., Quessy J. and Rémillard B. (2006a). 'Goodness-of-fit procedures for copula models based on the probability integral transformation'. *Scandinavian Journal of Statistics*, **volume 33**, pages 337–366. DOI: 10.1111/j.1467-9469.2006.00470.x. Cited on page 88.

Genest C. and Rémillard B. (2004). 'Tests of independence and randomness based on the empirical copula process'. *TEST*, **volume 13**, no. 2, pages 335–369. DOI: 10.1007/BF02595777. Cited on page 86.

Genest C., Rémillard B. and Beaudoin D. (2006b). 'Omnibus goodness-of-fit tests for copulas: A review and a power study'. URL: http://www.gerad.ca/fichiers/cahiers/G-2006-74.pdf. Cited on page 94.

Genest C. and Rivest L. (1993). 'Statistical inference procedures for bivariate Archimedean copulas'. *American Statistical Association*, **volume 88**, pages 1034–1043. DOI: 10.2307/2290796. Cited on page 75.

Genz A., Bretz F. and port by Torsten Hothorn R. (2006). *mvtnorm: Multivariate Normal and T Distribution*. R package version 0.7-5. Cited on page 2.

Gross J. (2003). *nortest: Tests for Normality*. R package version 1.0. Cited on page 2.

de Haan L. and Ferreira A. (2006). *Extreme Value Theory: An Introduction*. Springer. Cited on pages 16, 17, 18 and 19.

Harrell Jr. E.F. (2007). *Hmisc: Harrell Miscellaneous*. URL: http://biostat.mc.vanderbilt.edu/twiki/bin/view/Main/Hmisc. R package version 3.2-1. Cited on page 2.

Holland P.W. and Wang Y.J. (1987). 'Dependence functions for continuous bivariate densities'. *Communications in Statistics: Theory and Methods*, **volume 16**, no. 3, pages 863–876. ISSN 0361-0926. Cited on page 28.

Hufthammer K.O. (2005). *Some measures of local and global dependence*. Master's thesis, University of Bergen. URL: http://hdl.handle.net/1956/1066. Cited on pages 22 and 28.

Joe H. (1997). *Multivariate models and dependence concepts*, volume 73 of *Monographs on Statistics and Applied Probability*. Chapman & Hall. ISBN 0-412-07331-5. Cited on pages 3 and 79.

Joe H. and Xu J. (1996). 'The estimation method of inference functions for margins for multivariate models'. *Technical report*. Chapter 10 in Joe (1997). Cited on page 79.

Johnson R.A. and Wichern D.W. (2002). *Applied Multivariate Statistical Analysis*. Prentice Hall, Inc., fifth edition. Cited on page 3.

Jones M.C. and Koch I. (2003). 'Dependence maps: Local dependence in practice'. *Statistics and Computing*, **volume 13**, no. 3, pages 241–255. ISSN 0960-3174. DOI: 10.1023/A:1024270700807. Cited on page 28.

Kimberling C.H. (1974). 'A probabilistic interpretation of complete monotonicity'. *Aequationes Mathematicae,* **volume 10**, no. 2, pages 152–164. DOI: 10.1007/BF01832852. Cited on pages 45 and 53.

Li D. (2001). 'On default correlation: A copula function approach'. *Journal of Fixed Income,* **volume 9**, no. 4, pages 43–54. DOI: 10.2139/ssrn.187289. Cited on page 99.

Ligges U. and Mächler M. (2003). *Scatterplot3d - an R Package for Visualizing Multivariate Data.* URL: http://www.jstatsoft.org. Cited on page 2.

Lindskog F., McNeil A. and Schmock U. (2003). 'Kendall's tau for elliptical distributions'. In Bol G., Nakhaeizadeh G., Rachev S., Ridder T. and Vollmer K.H. (editors), 'Credit Risk: Measurement, Evaluation and Management', pages 149–156. Physica-Verlag Heidelberg. Cited on pages 33, 62, 64 and 75.

McNeil A.J., Frey R. and Embrechts P. (2005). *Quantitative risk management: Concepts, techniques and tools.* Princeton Series in Finance. Princeton University Press. ISBN 0-691-12255-5. Cited on pages 3, 9, 12, 14, 16, 17, 23, 25, 26, 33, 45, 52, 56, 57, 62, 65, 68, 74, 96 and 103.

Merton R. (1974). 'On the pricing of corporate debt: The risk structure of interest rates'. *The Journal of Finance,* **volume 29**, no. 2, pages 449–470. URL: http://hdl.handle.net/1721.1/1874. Cited on page 95.

Nelsen R.B. (2006). *An introduction to copulas.* Springer Series in Statistics. Springer, second edition. ISBN 978-0387-28659-4. Cited on pages 25, 34, 36, 39, 45, 46, 53, 59, 63, 85, 102 and 104.

R Development Core Team (2007). *R: A Language and Environment for Statistical Computing.* R Foundation for Statistical Computing, Vienna, Austria. URL: http://www.R-project.org. ISBN 3-900051-07-0. Cited on page 2.

Rosenblatt M. (1952). 'Remarks on a mulitvariate transformation'. *The Annals of Mathematical Statistics,* **volume 23**, no. 3, pages 470–472. Cited on pages 88 and 89.

Schweizer B. and Sklar A. (1983). *Probabilistic Metric Spaces.* North Holland. Cited on pages 36 and 39.

Skaug H. and Tjøstheim D. (1996). 'Testing for serial independence using measures of distance between densities'. In Robinson P. and Rosenblatt M. (editors), 'Athens Conference on Applied Probability and Time Series Analysis', volume 115 of *Lecture Notes in Statistics*, pages 363–378. Springer. Cited on page 93.

Sklar A. (1959). 'Fonctions de répartition à n dimensions et leurs marges'. *Publications de l'Institut de Statistique de l'Université de Paris*, **volume 8**, pages 229–231. Cited on pages 33 and 39.

Yan J. (2007). *Copula: Multivariate Dependence with Copula*. R package version 0.3-10. Cited on page 2.